The Resurrection Promise
AN INTERPRETATION
OF THE EASTER NARRATIVES

CHARLES AUSTIN PERRY

WILLIAM B. EERDMANS PUBLISHING COMPANY
GRAND RAPIDS, MICHIGAN

Library of Congress Cataloging-in-Publication Data

Perry, Charles A., 1928-
    The resurrection promise.

    Bibliography: p. 135
    1. Jesus Christ—Resurrection—Biblical teaching.
2. Bible. N.T. Gospels—Criticism, interpretation,
etc. 3. Jesus Christ—Resurrection—Sermons.
4. Sermons, American. 5. Episcopal Church—Sermons.
6. Anglican Communion—Sermons. I. Title.
BT481.P49   1986   232.9'7   86-24344

ISBN 0-8028-0249-4

Unless otherwise noted, all biblical quotations are from the Revised Standard Version of the Bible, copyrighted 1946, 1952, 1971, 1973.

ACKNOWLEDGMENTS

I am most grateful to Bishop Walker and the Chapter of Washington Cathedral, who provided me with a sabbatical, and to Dean William S. Pregnall and the Church Divinity School of the Pacific for the semester appointment as visiting scholar. With ample free time and the stimulating atmosphere of the Graduate Theological Union in Berkeley, California, I was able to get down to serious work on a theme that has long been of utmost concern to me. While I was there, two faculty members encouraged me and provided helpful comments on my manuscript: Dr. William L. Countryman of C.D.S.P., and Dr. Herman J. Waetjen of San Francisco Theological Seminary. The latter's seminar on "Death and Resurrection in the New Testament" was to provide a weekly stimulus. Doctoral candidates Father Scott G. Sinclair and Father Michael Gallagher, S.J., helped me with Greek and offered a number of suggestions.

Back in Washington, a number of readers offered editorial comments: the Reverend William Sydnor, the Reverend Dr. R. Taylor Scott, Ms. Nancy S. Montgomery, and Ms. Verna Dozier. My assistant and secretary, Ms. Betty Geisler, labored through numerous revisions.

The greatest source of support was my wife, Joy, who encouraged me in the first instance to write the book, acted as a library research assistant, and kept me going when the work bogged down. The book is my responsibility, but without these thoughtful persons it could not have come into being.

Contents

Dedication

In thanksgiving for a teacher who has most profoundly influenced my way of knowing my God and my world. The Reverend Dr. Clifford L. Stanley taught me at Virginia Theological Seminary to think theologically and to care deeply about the theological quest. He encouraged me to pursue ideas that twenty-five years later have resulted in this book.

Preface

All my life I have been part of a creedal church, the Protestant Episcopal Church. As I have participated in public worship, in common prayer, I have recited my belief in the resurrection of Jesus Christ and in the coming resurrection perhaps two or three thousand times. "The third day he rose again in accordance with the Scriptures" and "I look for the resurrection of the dead" I have said Sunday after Sunday. Ever since encountering modern science as a school child, I have been bothered by what I have recited, and at times, both as boy and as man, I have remained silent when the familiar creedal clauses came to my mind.

From the time I entered theological seminary twenty-eight years ago, I have been conscious of a responsibility to teach others about this strange and central—in fact, critical—belief of ours in the resurrection. Teaching and preaching about the Easter event and its meaning for us has been for me a preoccupation. In small rural parishes, in sophisticated college-town churches, and now in the National Cathedral of the Episcopal Church, I have talked and listened, sharing my belief and my doubts and hearing the perplexities of others.

The vast majority of practicing Christians are creedal. They profess belief in the resurrection of Jesus and in the coming resurrection, as do millions of evangelicals who accept the "fundamentals." My experience of more than forty years as an adult Christian and of more than twenty-five years as an ordained minister tells me that this profession of belief is not without considerable disbelief. Some Christians doggedly recite the church's formularies and try not to think about it. Others do what the church does and say what the church says only because being a Christian is very important to them. However, they harbor a personal skepticism about the resurrection event. They hope that the resurrection is not too important to the faith, and of course it is. Still others believe naively even though in other sectors of their intellectual life they are quite sophisticated. For them compartmentalism is necessary for personal integrity. Yet others are persistent inquirers, always asking and probing, sometimes believing, sometimes doubting. Many have arrived at an understanding of the resurrection with which they are comfortable. They are truly blessed, but who knows what sermon or article or experience may come to shake their comfort? Others have dropped out all together.

This is the church as I know it. It does not describe everyone, but it is the church in which I live and for which I care and for whom I write.

As I think back over the feedback I have received from the sermons I have preached and the classes I have taught, I hear the same questions asked over and over again: "Do you really believe that Jesus walked out of that tomb? Am I supposed to believe that I, too, will get a new body and join my loved ones who have died before me—and when will that happen?" When I preach or teach about the Easter texts, I am asked, "Do you really believe that Jesus walked through doors and ate fish and talked with his disciples?" But even more troubling is this type of question: "Oh, I guess I can believe that Jesus rose from the dead, but what difference does it make to me? It just seems rather unimportant to me and rather unrelated to life." I am asked such questions by the daring souls; I am sure there are countless others who are equally troubled but who won't ask.

One time, as a newly arrived rector in a Midwestern parish, I was in the process of visiting older parishioners who had drifted away from the church. Parish leaders said that the church's involvement in controversial social issues had driven them away. I asked each one I visited to tell me why she or he was remaining outside the church. A number said something like this: "When my husband [or wife] died, I stopped attending church. I just didn't believe any more and no longer needed to pretend. I'm too old for that." The church simply had not met their spiritual needs, including

their need to understand the church's belief and relate it to
their aging and their grief.

The questions are definitely out there. I can't prove how
pervasive they actually are, but my experience tells me that
a majority of the Christians among whom I have moved are
troubled and perplexed about the resurrection and are
having difficulty making any connection between the Easter Gospels, the creedal affirmations, and their lives. It is
for these that I write, though I hope that other, more settled
folk might enjoy joining me in this exploration as well.

This will be an inquiry into the Easter narratives, those
mysterious, enigmatic stories of the appearances among the
disciples of Jesus, risen and re-created as Lord and Christ. I
will take these stories seriously, very seriously indeed, for
every detail and utterance is special. I will ask what these
rather disparate stories have in common with each other. I
will ask what they can possibly have to do with our lives and
with what it means to profess belief in Christ Risen. There
will be inquiry into what happened and the meaning of it
for those early apostolic witnesses who were there. I will ask
what their encounter with Jesus, whom they knew as Lord,
meant to them, and further, what the evangelist is trying to
tell us about what it meant to him and to his community.

All this will be based on a conviction that the meaning of
the earliest encounters with the Living Lord illuminates the
meaning of our encounters with him today. In various ways
we Christians experience his presence today: in the midst of
the church assembled in his name, in our individual lives,
and in our going out into the world in his name to those in
need. Our experience and the biblical experience should
illuminate and interpret one another, or something is sadly
amiss.

I believe that the Easter narratives are especially precious
because they are very enlightening. I see a pattern that runs
through some of them, and that pattern, as I will try to
show, can be a paradigm for our self-understanding. The
pattern concerns Christ's presence and his command to go
out into the world as his disciples and his promise to be with

us as we go. The pattern also concerns our response to his presence in worship and adoration, to his command in obedience, and to his promise in trust. This stance of worship and obedience and trust is what I understand faith to be about, and it is brought about by his presence with us, his command of us and his promise to us. I am fully aware that talk of "patterns" in Scripture bothers many contemporary biblical interpreters. They think of harmonizations of Scripture that they thought they had left far behind. A brief word to them is in order here. This inquiry takes most seriously and appreciatively the work of the biblical form critics whose labor from the 1920s through 1960s was so important. They saw Scripture such as the Easter stories as small building blocks which, over time, through various editings, moved from oral to written tradition. By far the best current work in English on the resurrection narratives by a form critic is *The Formation of the Resurrection Narratives* by Reginald Fuller, originally published in 1971 and still available.

Since 1960, biblical criticism has turned increasingly to the examination of each Gospel as a whole. The scholars doing this work, known as redaction critics, want to know primarily what Matthew or John did with those earlier traditions that each inherited. There is an excellent work in English from this school as well: *The Easter Gospels: The Resurrection of Jesus According to the Four Evangelists* by Robert H. Smith, published in 1983.

I am grateful to both the form and the redaction critics, and to Fuller and Smith in particular. I have no intention of—nor capacity for—duplicating their work. Rather, what I see as a pattern in some of the appearance narratives is rooted in form criticism. It is not a harmonization but proceeds from a premise: that the disciples' actual experience of the presence of Jesus as Lord among them is what brings the several narratives into relationship. To encounter Jesus as risen provides unity amid the diversity of narratives. It—the seminal encounter—has an intrinsic pattern, a structure that we can see through the eyes of the several evangelists.

Despite differences in time and place of writing and in theological perspective, the pattern persists, even though there is little literary dependency. In my opinion, this pattern is a paradigm for our understanding our experience of him today in our midst.

We are participants in a tradition that proclaims a new creation, and our participation is informed by that of the apostolic witnesses because it is dependent on their testimony. We have their stories in the New Testament as mediated by the church of the first few generations. My hope is that this inquiry may contribute to both our understanding and our appreciation of the scriptural witness and to our understanding of ourselves as new creations with Christ.

CHAPTER 1

On the Third Day He Rose Again

INTRODUCTION: NO RESURRECTION, NO FAITH

There is no Christian faith without the resurrection. There may be a fine ethical religion with Jesus of Nazareth at the center, but it is not the biblical faith without the resurrection. The creeds of the church reflect quite accurately the preaching of the early church found throughout the New Testament and put most succinctly by Paul in his first letter to the Corinthians. In the fifteenth chapter he reminded the church at Corinth of the good news he had preached to them: "For I delivered to you as of first importance what I also received, that Christ died for our sins in accordance with the scriptures, that he was buried, that he was raised on the third day in accordance with the scriptures . . ." (vv. 3-4). The Corinthians, while they accepted the resurrection of Jesus, were questioning the resurrection of the dead (the general resurrection at the end of time). To them Paul wrote these emphatic words: "Now if Christ is preached as raised from the dead, how can some of you say that there is no resurrection of the dead? But if there is no resurrection of the dead, then Christ has not been raised; if Christ has not been raised, then our preaching is in vain and your faith is in vain" (vv. 12-14).

Paul's writings are consistent with the preaching of other early Christians as reflected in the New Testament. They proclaimed that God had raised Jesus from the dead, and they looked forward to participation in the resurrection at the close of the age (or the end of time). If Christ has not been raised, if there is no resurrection of the dead, then faith is empty. That is what the new community of Christians proclaimed, and that is what the early church councils set down in the creeds. No longer can we dodge the issue by distinguishing between a religion of Jesus and a religion of Saint Paul. Twentieth-century biblical scholarship has closed that door. If we want to believe what the early church proclaimed, then we cannot dispense with the resurrection.

BUT CAN WE BELIEVE? HISTORICAL AND SCIENTIFIC CONSIDERATIONS

But what is it that we are being asked to believe? What does it mean to say that Jesus rose (or, better, "was raised") from the dead? What does it mean to say that we will be raised from the dead? The Corinthian Christians asked, "How are the dead raised? With what kind of body do they come?" (1 Cor. 15:35). Paul called them "foolish" for asking. Most of us are still asking the same questions (and here I part with Paul), and we should not feel foolish in asking. We want to believe, but can we?

It is commonplace to say that modern science, natural and historical, has eroded our belief in the resurrection. From the time of the Enlightenment many scholars and common folk have publicly questioned the truth of the resurrection, and even some public figures like Thomas Jefferson have audaciously excised the Easter narratives from their Bibles. I will not recite the long history of growing skepticism and the heroic attempts of nineteenth-century theologians and biblical scholars to come up with a "rational" statement of the resurrection. They raised the right questions, although their answers satisfy few today.

In our times many scholars wrestling with questions inherited from the past have concluded that we "can't" go beyond the faith of the church, or that we "shouldn't" go beyond it or we "don't need to" go beyond it. Instead we should have faith in the Easter proclamation and not bother ourselves with the question of what actually happened to give rise to the Easter faith. In their view, the Easter narratives are so layered with myth and legend that they are of little historical value. I find this all very unsatisfactory. We have prided ourselves on being "an historic faith," yet we don't wish to investigate the event that brought us into being with the tools of the historian. I agree with the point made by English bishop and New Testament scholar J. A. T. Robinson in *Can We Trust the New Testament?*:

> If the resurrection story has a foot in *public* history (and to abandon that claim is to abandon something that has been central to the entire Christian tradition), then it must be open and vulnerable to the historian's scrutiny. . . . And though the historian can neither give nor directly take away the faith, he can indirectly render the credibility-gap so wide that in fact men cease believing. My trust in the New Testament accepts that risk. That is why as a New Testament scholar I am convinced that it is important to be a good historian as well as a man of faith—and not to confuse the two by giving answers of faith where historical evidence alone is relevant. For *if* Jesus could really be shown to be the sort of man who went into hiding rather than face death, or just another nationalist or freedom-fighter with a crime-sheet of violence, or the leader of a movement which rested in the last analysis on fraud, then I can think of other candidates in reply to Peter's question, "Lord, to whom else shall we go?" (John 6.68). The answers that history can give will never take us all the way—and at best they cannot be more than highly probable. Exactly what happened at the tomb, or anywhere else, we shall never know. All we can ask—and must require—for faith, for the response of Thomas, "My Lord and my God!", is that the credibility-gap be not too wide. And that assurance I am persuaded—or I would not remain a Christian—is what the history, after all the sifting of the best and most rigorous scholarship, can sustain.[1]

1. Robinson, *Can We Trust the New Testament?* (Grand Rapids: Eerdmans, 1977), pp. 128-29.

So let us proceed with the historical investigation. Even the most skeptical historians would agree that something happened in the first century of our era sufficient to cause a small band of Jews in Palestine of modest education and status to proclaim, in the face of great odds, what was heresy to the Jews, and to initiate a major schism within Judaism. If we accept the crucifixion of their leader Jesus as a fact (and even most skeptics do) the small band of followers of the Rabbi from Nazareth had every reason to flee in fear (and that is what the biblical record says [John 20:19; Mark 14:50; Matt. 26:56b] despite the obvious embarrassment it must have caused the leaders of the new movement). There is little challenge to the conclusion that something drastic happened in the lives of Jesus' followers after his death and burial.

The question is, What happened and how can we know that it happened? The first Christians accounted for their radically changed behavior by saying "Jesus is Lord" and "God has raised Jesus." John H. Hick, a contemporary British philosopher, says of this about-face,

So long as we do not insist upon any dogmatic definition of its precise nature, we can assert that beyond all reasonable doubt what has come to be called "the resurrection of Jesus" was a real occurrence. For it can hardly be questioned that something immensely impressive, and in that sense undeniably real, happened shortly after Jesus' death to restore and enhance his disciples' faith in him as their living Lord and Master. If their life-situation had not been transformed by some powerfully moving event it seems very unlikely that the tiny Jesus-movement within Judaism would long have survived the execution of its leader and that there would today, nearly two thousand years later, be a christian community numbering hundreds of millions.[2]

Many theologians and commentators want to stop right here. The only historic data, they say, is the faith of the early

2. Hick, *Death and Eternal Life* (New York: Harper & Row, 1976), p. 171.

church, and we don't have to go beyond it. Karl Barth, perhaps the leading Continental theologian of this century, would say on dogmatic grounds that Jesus really rose from the dead but that historical investigation cannot add anything to the proclamation of the church.[3] John Hick says that we don't need to go beyond the faith of the church:

> The resurrection may have been a bodily event, and the body may have mysteriously materialized and dematerialized; there may have been angels, earthquake and guards fainting; there may have been lengthy discourses by the risen Christ to his disciples, terminated after some weeks by his ascension into the air. But the gospel that Jesus lives, exalted by God to a glorious role in the process of man's salvation, does not depend upon the historicity of any of these problematic elements of the New Testament tradition.[4]

I agree with John Robinson that "the resurrection story has a foot in public history," and disagree with Hick on this point. But immediately a distinction must be made, a distinction between the resurrection of Jesus and the appearances of the Risen One to the disciples. The New Testament mentions no eyewitnesses to the resurrection of Jesus. Whatever happened to Jesus between the burial and the appearances of the exalted Lord is not described in the canonical Gospels. It is only inferred from the disciples' encounters with the Risen One and from the empty tomb. Walter Kunneth, a German theologian writing in *The Theology of the Resurrection,* says that the resurrection of Jesus could not have been witnessed because it is a "primal miracle" or act of God comparable and parallel to God's act of creation. Here, he says, we are speaking of an order or dimension of reality beyond space and time, one which therefore could not be observed within those limits. It is

---

3. See the discussion of Barth in Richard R. Niebuhr, *Resurrection and Historical Reason: A Study of Theological Method* (New York: Scribner's, 1957), pp. 42-51; and David McKenzie, *Wolfhart Pannenberg and Religious Philosophy* (Washington: University Press of America, 1980), p. 103n.2.

4. Hick, *Death and Eternal Life,* p. 177.

unique and beyond historical investigation.[5] I think that this distinction is tenable: the resurrection of Jesus per se is beyond history and therefore beyond historical investigation, but the appearances of the Risen One are within history and therefore subject to historical judgments of probability.

Kunneth believes that the word "reality" is appropriately used of the resurrection of Jesus and that this order or dimension of reality is not comprehended by the concept of myth, as so many commentators believe.[6] C. H. Dodd, the English New Testament critic, has investigated the appearance narratives and is in basic agreement with Kunneth regarding the use of the term "myth": "It has been not unusual to apply the term 'myth' somewhat loosely to the resurrection-narratives of the gospels as a whole. The foregoing investigation will have shown that, so far as the narratives of the appearances of the risen Christ are concerned, form-criticism offers no ground to justify the use of the term."[7]

Kunneth believes further that the concept of another dimension or order of reality that interacts with historical time and space is not incompatible with contemporary natural science. Many theologians have argued that modern science rules out such notions. To this he responds as follows:

> The world-picture of a mechanistic and materialistic science and the speculative world-view based upon it, to which Bultmann . . . [and others, I might add] appeals, is today at all events obsolete. The concepts of a universally calculable causal system and determinism which labels every extraordinary occurrence, such as miracle, as "breaking" the laws of nature, are in process of dissolution. Far more typical of the

5. Kunneth, *The Theology of the Resurrection* (London: SCM Press, 1965), pp. 72-78.

6. Kunneth, *The Theology of the Resurrection*, p. 62.

7. Dodd, "The Appearances of the Risen Christ: An Essay in Form-Criticism of the Gospels," in *More New Testament Studies* (Grand Rapids: Eerdmans, 1968), p. 133.

principles of scientific thinking today are the ideas of the "freedom" of natural phenomena and the "indeterminacy" of final patterns. According to the theories of this contemporary world-picture, we must reckon in principle with the breaking into the cosmos at any moment of new, perhaps hitherto unknown energies, and consequently with the alteration of present researches, judgments and laws.[8]

The concept of "myth" does not apply to the reality of the resurrection, nor does science rule out the resurrection. Neither does Kunneth's argument prove that the resurrection happened. It does, however, tend to clear away some obstacles in the way of Christians' reaching that conclusion.

RESURRECTION AS RE-CREATION

A theologian who agrees with Kunneth that natural science doesn't rule out the reality of the resurrection is Wolfhart Pannenberg. He goes further than Kunneth, believing that the resurrection is a historical event subject to historical investigation.[9] (His argument is summarized in Appendix 1.) However, Pannenberg believes with Kunneth that the actual resurrection of Jesus occurred outside the ken of human observation, and that since we have no empirical experience of resurrection per se, we can speak of it only metaphorically.[10] This is a most important observation. The Greek words translated by the Latin derivative "resurrection" (from *re surgere*—"to rise up again") literally denote "awakening" and "arising from sleep." In this metaphor, death is likened to sleep. The Greek words *anistēmi* and *egeirō*, which are translated by "resurrection," refer to "rising" from sleep. Saint Paul is aware of the inadequacy of language in talking about this unique and unprecedented event, but for us "resurrection" has become a technical term

8. Kunneth, *The Theology of the Resurrection,* p. 66.
9. Pannenberg, *Jesus—God and Man* (Philadelphia: Westminster Press, 1968), pp. 88ff.
10. Pannenberg, *Jesus—God and Man,* p. 74.

used a bit too literally. It refers obviously to a transformation or metamorphosis of Jesus, effected by God, from an
earthly and perishable body to what Paul refers to as a
"spiritual body." The first died on the cross, and the second
is a new creation. The two are related in that the spiritual
body of the Risen One can be identified with Jesus of Nazareth, who was crucified.

It is important to be able to come to the concept of resurrection with an open mind, and to facilitate this I will use
another word to point to that which God accomplished in
Jesus and will accomplish for us at the end of time. For this
act that Kunneth has pointed out is comparable and parallel
to God's original act of creation, I will use "re-creation." I
believe that I am on solid biblical ground in such a use. Paul
speaks of Jesus Christ as the "second Adam" and of those
who participate in his life, who are in him, as a "new creation." That order or dispensation that will replace this one is
called "a new heaven and a new earth" in Revelation. Exam-
ples could be multiplied, but let me simply stipulate that
"re-creation" will be used throughout the book to mean
"resurrection." This word stresses newness and rebirth,
and thus does not emphasize the rising of a physical body in
time and space but instead points to God's mysterious act of
beginning again.

CONCLUSION

A church came into being, and it testified that God had
raised Jesus and that its claim was based on a series of encounters with One whom they knew as both Jesus who was
crucified and the Lord who was present to them. The memory of these encounters is set forth in the New Testament.
We can apply the most rigorous historical scholarship to the
record of that memory, but we also read it in the midst of
our worship. We know that the church's memory as set
forth in Scripture does not include God's act of re-creation
itself but only the encounter with the One who was created

anew. That act is beyond history, but his appearance "has a foot in public history." The category of myth seems inappropriate for understanding, but we must reckon with "resurrection" as a metaphor and hence will substitute the word "re-creation" to make that point.

I have concluded that neither natural nor historical science can exclude the re-creation, nor can either be used to prove it. We are free to take seriously the details of the record of the church's memory without ruling out the details on some *a priori* basis. The early church's account seems to me to be plausible, credible, and intelligible (but not all has been said on that point). However, this witness can't "prove" the re-creation to an impartial observer, although reasoning about the re-creation can make such an observer receptive to faith. It is not, therefore, reason or revelation, not historical reason or faith, but reason *and* revelation and historical reasoning *and* faith. The first prepares the way for the second, or at least removes impediments from the path of faith. Reason operates within faith, and faith gives us reason to reason. We shall see that reasoning about the Easter encounters with Jesus as Lord helps us to understand not only the nature of the formative events but also the nature of faith itself, for the experience of re-creation then and now is at the center of faith. In faith and with reason we can better understand the record of the earliest experiences of Jesus as Lord, and in so doing better comprehend our own experience of him.

Join me now as I attempt to reconstruct what happened in that crucial moment of history we call Easter. Let us begin with Paul on the Damascus road.

CHAPTER 2

Last of All, as to One Untimely Born, He Appeared Also to Me
1 CORINTHIANS 15:8

Mainstream New Testament criticism concludes that Saint Paul, writing in the fifteenth chapter of 1 Corinthians, gives us the earliest written summary of the church's belief about the re-creation.[1] Paul writes, probably in A.D. 55, "For I delivered to you as of first importance what I also received, that Christ died for our sins in accordance with the scriptures, that he was buried, that he was raised on the third day in accordance with the scriptures . . ." (vv. 3-4). Such a summary is found in somewhat different form in the sermons attributed to Peter in Acts (2:22ff., 3:12ff.) and elsewhere in the New Testament.

To this summary that Paul tells us he "received," he appends a list of appearances of the Lord: ". . . and that he appeared to Cephas, then to the twelve. Then he appeared to more than five hundred brethren at one time, most of whom are still alive, though some have fallen asleep. Then he appeared to James, then to all the apostles. Last of all, as to one untimely born, he appeared also to me" (vv. 5-8). Paul may have used this list to substantiate the core of the Gospel message or "kerygma" in verses 3-4, or he may have used it to substantiate his claim to be an apostle, just like Peter and James and the rest, or he may have used it for both purposes. In any event, this list is our earliest written account of the appearances of our Lord to the first Christians.

It is not my purpose here to attempt to review the volu-

1. Reginald H. Fuller, *The Formation of the Resurrection Narratives* (New York: Macmillan, 1971), pp. 9ff., 48.

minous commentary on these critical verses of Saint Paul,[2] nor to try to match up the appearances listed by Paul with those narrated in the Gospels. Rather, I wish to consider the appearance of Christ to Paul himself and the language Paul used to describe that experience. My intention is to shed light on Christ's appearances in the Gospels, which is my central concern.

Paul, writing about twenty-five years after the crucifixion, presents the list of Christ's appearances in a very matter-of-fact way. We know from Paul's letters that he had met with James and Peter (Cephas). Presumably, he had heard their firsthand reports of the Lord's appearance to them. His reference to the five hundred, "most of whom are still alive," certainly implies his acquaintance with at least some of them also. Furthermore, it requires no stretch of the imagination to conclude that one who has met with James and Peter and who has traveled widely has heard directly from eyewitnesses the accounts of the appearance(s) to "the twelve" and "all the apostles."

What is important to us here is that Paul lists the appearance of the Lord to himself right along with these earlier appearances witnessed by others. It is our only firsthand account of the Lord's appearance. Paul makes no apparent distinction in quality or importance between the appearance to himself and those "to the twelve," who had been with Jesus prior to the crucifixion. He regards his experience as equivalent to theirs.[3] The only distinction he makes is in the words "last of all, as to one untimely born." "Last of all" might simply mean that Christ had appeared most recently to Paul or that his final appearance was to Paul. If the latter, it could mean simply that Paul had heard

2. For a very full treatment of 1 Corinthians 15, see Hans Conzelmann, *First Corinthians: A Critical and Historical Commentary on the Bible,* trans. James W. Leitch, ed. George W. MacRae (Philadelphia: Fortress Press, 1975), pp. 248-93.

3. Fuller, *The Formation of the Resurrection Narratives,* pp. 29-30, 43-44; and James D. G. Dunn, *Jesus and the Spirit: A Study of the Religious and Charismatic Experience of Jesus and the First Christians as Reflected in the New Testament* (Philadelphia: Westminster Press, 1975), pp. 100-103.

of no appearances between his conversion (perhaps three to five years after the crucifixion) and the time of writing (probably twenty-five years after). Alternatively, it could mean that the appearances necessarily came to a close in short compass with the conversion of the apostle to the Gentiles.[4] Again, Paul is not giving his encounter with Jesus re-created as Lord a second-class status compared with the others he lists. Only in the enigmatic reference "as to one untimely born" do we have any depreciation of his position. The Greek, *ektrōmati*, means literally "abortion." Paul, characterizing himself as a "monstrosity," perhaps because he had been a persecutor of the church, was graced by the appearance of the Lord as were those far worthier than he.

Let us look more closely at the appearance to Paul. We find that he says very little about it. Here he simply uses the word *ōphthē*, which can be translated "appeared" or "was seen," the same word he uses for the encounters of the others before him. In describing his calling (Gal. 1:11-17), he refers to himself as one who "persecuted the church of God violently and tried to destroy it," and then says, "But when he who had set me apart before I was born and had called me through his grace, was pleased to reveal *(apocalypsai)* his Son to me (literally, 'in me'), in order that I might preach him among the Gentiles . . ." (vv. 15-16). In this description the appearance is a "revelation," and "in me" may imply an inner spiritual revelation, not an appearance. Earlier in his first letter to the Corinthians (9:1), Paul asks, "Have I not seen *(heoraka)* Jesus our Lord?" These three are the only direct references he makes to his conversion experience. He gives no details, just three words, two forms of one verb referring to "seeing" and one to "revelation."

It may be helpful to take a closer look at the vocabulary Paul uses to describe the appearance to him of "Jesus our Lord." In 1 Corinthians Paul uses two forms of the verb "to see" *(oraō)*. This word as used in the New Testament and in

---

4. Fuller, *The Formation of the Resurrection Narratives*, p. 43; see also Dunn, *Jesus and the Spirit*, p. 101.

the Septuagint (the Greek version of the Old Testament) has a range of meanings, from sense perception to spiritual perception. It is filled with the ambiguity of the English word "to see." We use "to see" to mean "I perceive with my eyes" as well as "I understand" and also to denote insight, as in "I was blind to miss that, but now I see." Such "seeing" can refer both to a simple leap to intellectual understanding and to a deep spiritual understanding. Though not exactly equivalent to the English, the principal Greek word, *oraō*, has a similar range of meanings.

In the form used in 1 Corinthians 15, *ōpthē*, the word may simply denote presence, as in the translation "he appeared to." Nothing is necessarily implied about the visual content or mode of the appearance. Moreover, there is a considerable difference of opinion about the meaning of *oraō* when it is used in relation to the appearances. W. Michaelis in *The Theological Dictionary of the New Testament* says,

> When *ōpthē* is used as a tt. [technical term] to denote the resurrection appearances there is no primary emphasis on seeing as sensual or mental perception. The dominant thought is that the appearances are revelations, encounters with the risen Lord who herein reveals Himself, or is revealed. . . . He encountered them as the risen, living Lord; they experienced His presence. In the last resort even active terms like *heoraka* in 1 C. 9:1 means the same thing. . . . When Paul classifies the Damascus appearance with the others in 1 C. 15:5ff., this is not merely because he regards it as equivalent (especially in relation to his apostleship, and in spite of his own unworthiness, 15:8ff.). It is also because he regards this appearance as similar in kind. In all the appearances the presence of the risen Lord is a presence in transfigured corporeality, 1 C. 15:42ff. . . . This presence is in non-visionary reality; no category of human seeing is wholly adequate for it.[5]

5. Michaelis, "horáō C2," in *TDNT*, ed. Gerhard Kittel and Gerhard Friedrich, trans. Geoffrey W. Bromiley, 9 vols. (Grand Rapids: Eerdmans, 1964-1974), 5: 358-59.

Hans Conzelmann specifically disagrees with Michaelis: "What is meant [by Paul] is a real visible manifestation."[6] James D. G. Dunn in *Jesus and the Spirit* gives a very complete discussion of Paul's usage in particular. He concludes,

It must be emphasized that in the passages before us *ophtherai* can hardly have any other sense than visual perception. In biblical Greek *ophtherai* always denotes seeing with the eyes. This applies equally to seeing physical objects, theophanies, visions and dreams—the one who sees really sees. This is not of course to deny the revelatory character of the resurrection appearance to Paul, but simply to affirm that in I Cor. 15:8 as in I Cor. 9:1 Paul claims actually to have seen something.[7]

The question remains, What did Paul actually see? Dunn states, "The only answer that Paul allows us to give is 'Jesus.' And having said that we can say little more, for Paul nowhere describes what he saw—nor even attempts to do so."[8] In Dunn's view, Paul has not given much content to the verb "see." However, Dunn draws the following conclusion:

What we can say with more certainty is that Paul himself was convinced that what he saw was external to him—was Jesus alive from the dead, alive in a new mode of existence (spiritual body). This is apparent in Paul's use of *ōphthē*—the passive indicating that the initiative in the seeing lay not with the see-er but with the one seen—he appeared, showed himself to (dative), not he was seen by (*hupo*). It is "the one who appears" who acts, the person who receives the appearance is passive, he experiences the appearance. In this sense, such an experience means seeing something which is given to the seer to see.[9]

Paul's only other direct reference (Gal. 1:11-17) to the appearance of the Lord to him uses the word "revealed" (*apoc-*

6. Conzelmann, *First Corinthians,* p. 257n.74.
7. Dunn, *Jesus and the Spirit,* p. 105.
8. Dunn, *Jesus and the Spirit,* p. 106.
9. Dunn, *Jesus and the Spirit,* p. 108.

alypsai). His meeting with the Lord was a revelatory encounter. Again there is no description. While neither word gives us specific content to his experience of "seeing," Paul does distinguish elsewhere between visions and revelations on the one hand and the appearance of Jesus on the other. Robert H. Smith points out that "the former are private experiences and only the latter form the basis of his proclamation and ministry."[10] (See 2 Cor. 12:1ff. compared with 1 Cor. 9:1 and 15:8.) I would agree with Conzelmann and Dunn. Paul saw someone external to himself identified as Jesus our Lord. The initiative was clearly taken by the Lord Jesus, whom Paul had never met before.

Can the accounts in Acts of the appearance on the Damascus road add anything to Paul's most reserved descriptions of his conversion and call? Reginald Fuller believes that there may be elements in the three accounts in Acts (9:1-22; 22:3-21; and 26:1-23) that are earlier traditions that came to the author of Acts and are not incompatible with Paul's own references to his conversion: the light, the voice, and the concealment of the encounter from Paul's traveling companions.[11] But Paul says he saw "the Lord," not a "light." However, in 2 Corinthians 4:6 he does say, "For it is the God who said, 'Let light shine out of darkness,' who has shone in our hearts to give the light of the knowledge of the glory of God in the face of Christ." This may refer to his personal experience. Furthermore, Paul refers to the re-created body as "raised in glory," *doxē* (1 Cor. 15:43). "Glory" and "light" in Old Testament use are closely allied. Glory "shines." From these facts Fuller suggests "very tentatively, that the form which the self-disclosure of the Risen One took for Paul (and therefore presumably, also for the recipients of appearances prior to him) was the form of a vision of light."[12] Personally, I don't find it necessary to be so tentative about the Damascus ex-

10. Smith, *The Easter Gospels: The Resurrection of Jesus According to the Four Evangelists* (Minneapolis: Augsburg, 1983), p. 117.
11. Fuller, *The Formation of the Resurrection Narratives*, pp. 42ff.
12. Fuller, *The Formation of the Resurrection Narratives*, p. 47.

perience as described in Acts. Nevertheless, Paul's own writings are certainly the primary source. Further, though a blinding light accompanied by the commanding voice of Jesus may have been the form of the presence of Jesus as Lord that Paul encountered, it is not to be "presumed" that this was the "form of self-disclosure" for the recipients of appearances prior to Paul. The appearance narratives, as we will see later on, make no mention of light and do provide a great deal of additional content which should not be reduced to that of the version of Paul's encounter given in Acts.

Paul gives us further insight into the nature of the Re-created One whom he encountered. In the remainder of 1 Corinthians 15 he speculates about the nature of the resurrection (re-creation) that the faithful will experience. Though he does not say that he is describing the glorified body of Jesus, it seems reasonable to conclude that his speculation about our participation in the new creation could be influenced by the presence of Jesus re-created as Lord that he experienced. The Lord appeared to him, he "saw" the Lord, perhaps in or as a blinding light. He met the Lord in a glorified or transfigured state. Would not his language about our future existence, our re-created life, be affected by what he saw and heard? It should be noted, however, that Paul does not argue this way. In answer to the question "How are the dead raised? With what kind of body do they come?" (15:35), he does not say something like "with a body like that of Jesus, which I saw." Nevertheless, Paul does say directly that the "Savior, the Lord Jesus Christ, . . . will change our lowly body to be like his glorious body" (Phil. 3:20-21). Thus his description in 1 Corinthians 15 of the "body" with which we will be clothed should have some relationship to the "body" of the re-created Lord who appeared to him.

What is this "body" like? In a major section of the fifteenth chapter, Paul attempts to answer the question apparently asked by the Corinthians about the risen body. Paul uses the analogy of the kernel of grain dying (rotting) in the ground and coming to life again (vv. 36-38), thus implying both continuity and discontinuity. His readers knew that a particular seed yielded a particular plant (continuity). They also knew that the seed first rotted in the ground and that the plant was greatly different from the seed in appearance, size, and so on (discontinuity). They did not know the biological relationship between seed and plant as we do, but they would understand the analogy to imply both continuity and discontinuity. Paul then speaks of different kinds of flesh *(sarx)*—that of men, animals, birds, and fish— and different kinds of bodies *(sōmata):* terrestrial and celestial, each having its own "glory" (vv. 39-41). As these differ one from another, so does the spiritual body *(pneumatikon sōma)* differ from the physical body *(physikon sōma).* It is imperishable, not perishable; glorious, not dishonored; powerful, not weak. "Flesh and blood cannot inherit the kingdom of God" (v. 50) because it is perishable. The perishable body is "changed" (v. 51), changed from this body of death, which bears the image of the first Adam, to a spiritual body, which bears the image of Jesus Christ, the new Adam.

The Greek word for body *(sōma)* as used by Paul probably reflects Paul's Hebrew roots rather than the use of the Hellenistic community in which he traveled, though some commentators would disagree.[13] Hebrew did not have a single word for "body," but a plentitude of words were translated in the Septuagint by a few Greek words, principally *sōma* and *sarx* (usually translated "body" and "flesh"). Paul uses *sōma* to denote the whole person (physical, mental, and spiritual), not simply flesh in which dwells a soul (the Greek view). The whole person both is a body and has a body. We cannot know one without the other. My person is

13. See Ronald J. Sider, "The Pauline Conception of the Resurrection Body in I Cor. 15:35-54," *New Testament Studies* 21 (1974-75): 428-39. See also J. A. T. Robinson, *The Body: A Study in Pauline Theology,* Studies in Biblical Theology, no. 5 (London: SCM Press, 1952); and M. E. Dahl, *The Resurrection of the Body: A Study of I Corinthians 15,* Studies in Biblical Theology, no. 36 (London: SCM Press, 1962).

expressed through and by my body, and my body is the
form that communicates my person. They go together.
When I die, my body dies, but does my person die? Paul is
ambiguous on this point. Discontinuity seems to be implied
in 1 Corinthians 15, but in his second letter to the Corinthians he implies that there will be a personal continuity:
"For we know that if the earthly tent we live in is destroyed,
we have a building from God, a house not made with hands,
eternal in the heavens" (5:1). Apparently there will be continuity of personhood and identity for us as there was for
Jesus re-created as Lord. In any event, we are given a new
body in which our personal identity will be continued. The
new body results from a new act of creation, and it is
glorious and imperishable. In the original act of creation
God gave to each order its own appropriate body; in the re-
creation he will do no less. Humankind will be given a body
appropriate to the new creation—a spiritual body.[14]

From Paul's speculation about our future bodies, what
can we conclude about the body of Jesus re-created as
Lord? First, Christ's body is glorious. He reflects and manifests the glory of God. Second, it is spiritual. It is not limited
by the constraints of that which is earthly (both the constraints of time and space and the constraints of sin). Third,
it is imperishable; it will not die. Last, it exhibits continuity:
the glorified body of the One he called Lord is identified
with and as Jesus who was crucified. Paul knew that the One
he had encountered, who appeared to him, was "Jesus our
Lord" (1 Cor. 9:1), despite the fact that he had never met
Jesus of Nazareth.

There was identity or continuity: the Lord was known to
be Jesus. But there was also discontinuity: the Lord Jesus
had not an earthly body but a glorious body, a spiritual body
as we will one day have. The author of Acts is quite consistent with Paul's own writing when he depicts in Acts 9 the
continuity—"I am Jesus, whom you are persecuting"

---

14. Pheme Perkins, *Resurrection: New Testament Witness and Contemporary Reflection* (Garden City, N.Y.: Doubleday, 1984), p. 304.

(v. 5)—and the discontinuity: "and suddenly a light from heaven flashed about him" (v. 3). The more corporeal body that the Gospel narratives intimate, particularly the later ones, is not described here. However, the glorified Lord was present to Paul and was identified as Jesus of the cross. He commanded Paul to go to Damascus and to do what he was told. When in the Acts narrative Paul goes to that city, he meets a man—Ananias—who conveys to him the promise that he will "be filled with the Holy Spirit." This three-fold pattern (presence, command, and promise) is what we shall perceive in the appearance narratives to be discussed later.

However, my purpose here has been to describe Paul's encounter primarily from his letters rather than from the story in Acts. By so doing I hope to have illuminated this "last" encounter with the re-created Lord, the first to show up in written form, and to have laid a foundation that will be useful in later discussions. I should note the obvious: seeing the Lord turned Paul's life around. The persecutor became the champion. He became a man with a new mission, which he attributed clearly to "seeing" the Lord. The Damascus road experience was for him a commissioning: God "was pleased to reveal his Son to me, in order that I might preach him among the Gentiles" (Gal. 1:16). Paul understood himself to be sent to proclaim the good news that he received when he "saw the Lord," that others might hear and believe: "And how are they to believe in him of whom they have never heard? . . . And how can men preach unless they are sent? . . . Faith comes from what is heard" (Rom. 10:14b-15a, 17).

CHAPTER 3

Encounters at the Tomb

The earliest written tradition in the Gospels that speaks of events that transpire after the death and burial of Jesus is found in the eight verses that bring Mark's Gospel to a close (16:1-8). In this terse account the Lord does not appear. There is no encounter with the second Adam, Jesus, who can now be called Christ. What we have is a negative statement, an empty tomb. This book derives its thesis and reaches its conclusions from an examination of the appearance narratives, which will be our main concern. But we cannot ignore the end of Mark's Gospel, for there it stands, the earliest written Gospel ending, though probably not the oldest written tradition of the postcrucifixion events, as we have noted in the previous chapter on Paul.

It is believed that traditions of the appearances and the empty tomb circulated (probably independently) in oral form, and perhaps in writing, from a very early date.[1] (I would say of the oral traditions, "from the beginning.") In written form the earliest narrative of the empty-tomb tradition is found in Mark (ca. A.D. 70), written about fifteen years after Paul's first letter to the Corinthians. This does not mean—though it seems to be forgotten from time to time by scholars—that the Pauline tradition is necessarily older. The empty-tomb narrative may have circulated in oral form at an earlier date.

The empty-tomb narratives in the other three Gospels were written later than Mark, and those in Matthew and

---

1. See J. A. T. Robinson, *Can We Trust the New Testament?* (Grand Rapids: Eerdmans, 1977); Reginald H. Fuller, *The Formation of the Resurrection Narratives* (New York: Macmillan, 1971); and Pheme Perkins, *Resurrection: New Testament Witness and Contemporary Reflection* (Garden City, N.Y.: Doubleday, 1984).

Luke are dependent on Mark. I should add, however, that Matthew and Luke diverge at many points from Mark in their telling of the story of the women at the tomb, and John, as usual, is in a different world altogether. When I discuss the appearances, it will be necessary to look at most of the narratives separately, but in the case of the empty tomb I will examine only the Markan narrative in detail, with some references to the differences found in the other three. The Markan text is as follows:

> And when the sabbath was past, Mary Magdalene, and Mary the mother of James, and Salome, bought spices, so that they might go and anoint him. And very early on the first day of the week they went to the tomb when the sun had risen. And they were saying to one another, "Who will roll away the stone for us from the door of the tomb?" And looking up, they saw that the stone was rolled back—it was very large. And entering the tomb, they saw a young man sitting on the right side, dressed in a white robe; and they were amazed. And he said to them, "Do not be amazed; you seek Jesus of Nazareth, who was crucified. He has risen, he is not here; see the place where they laid him. But go, tell his disciples and Peter that he is going before you to Galilee; there you will see him, as he told you." And they went out and fled from the tomb; for trembling and astonishment had come upon them; and they said nothing to any one, for they were afraid. (16:1-8)

It should be noted that the best manuscripts of the Gos-pel of Mark end with verse eight, and contain no account of the appearance of the re-created Lord Christ. There are texts that are quite late that are purported to be the "lost ending," but few scholars accept them as such, and the Re-vised Standard Version includes the text only as a footnote. Was there an appearance narrative with a longer ending? There is no agreement, and the argument is not germane to my thesis.

What is going on in the narratives of the women at the tomb? The disciples have fled Jerusalem according to the

passion tradition. Women alone among Jesus' followers
stood by at the end, though at a distance. On the morning of
the first day of the week, probably "the third day" of the
predictions, they go to the tomb to anoint the body properly
for burial or perhaps just to view the grave. They are aware
that the grave was sealed with a large stone, and to their
surprise it has been moved aside, so they go inside (though
not according to Matthew). There they have an encounter
that leaves them beside themselves (literally "ecstatic"), as-
tonished and trembling. They hear a proclamation: "You
seek Jesus of Nazareth, who was crucified. He has risen (or,
better, 'he was raised'), he is not here." The Lukan version
of the proclamation is "Why do you seek the living among
the dead? Remember how he told you, while he was still in
Galilee, that the Son of Man must be delivered into the
hands of sinful men, and be crucified, and on the third day
rise" (24:5-7). In the tomb, in the place of death and with no
expectation of anything but defeat, they hear a message of
triumph. He is not dead, but living. He is not in the tomb,
but risen, as he had told them in Galilee he would be. This is
the message that they hear, though in written form as we
have it, it resembles closely the Gospel in miniature that
Paul sets forth in 1 Corinthians.

We are told by the narrator that the women's experience
is dramatic and shaking. It upsets all their expectations.
What they hear cuts to the core of their being. So does what
they see. Luke and John tell us that those who enter the
tomb find it empty; presumably they all saw that it was
empty. They heard a voice telling them the good news of
why it was empty. Mark, Matthew, and Luke describe the
scene in traditional biblical terms. When a message of such
profound import comes to a human from God, it is usually
through a messenger. Mark is ambiguous in his language.
The messenger is "a young man," but his clothing is that of
God's messenger. Luke tells us there are two "men" but
later (24:23) refers to "a vision of angels," and Matthew tells
us of an "angel." The important point is that the women saw

that the tomb was empty, and they knew that Jesus, who was crucified and died and was buried, had risen and now lived.

The message included not only an affirmation of the re-creation of Jesus, now Lord and Christ, but a command to "go and tell." They were to be "goers," those who are sent, and "tellers." Women—whose testimony could not be used in court and who were therefore suspect witnesses—were commissioned in this divine encounter with this most precious of all messages. However, they were to go and tell the disciples, not the world. The individual evangelists offer different renderings of the message entrusted to the women by the heavenly messenger. According to Mark, the women were told that "He has risen" and were told to "tell his disciples and Peter that he is going before you to Galilee; there you will see him, as he told you" (16:7). Matthew adds that the angelic message is to include "that he has risen from the dead" (28:7), but here also the women are to go and tell the disciples, presumably not the world. Luke includes a bit more of the kerygma in the message (24:6-7) without limiting the women's intended audience, and subsequently the women tell "all this to the eleven and to all the rest" (24:9). According to John, there is no heavenly messenger, and Mary Magdalene alone finds the tomb empty and runs to tell Peter and the Beloved Disciple.

So the mission of the women according to Mark and Matthew appears limited to witnessing to the disciples about the empty tomb. They are not commanded, as are the disciples, to tell "all nations" that Jesus has risen. However, entrusting to women even a circumscribed message intended for a limited audience is astounding and without precedent, and women in the first century would have been aware of this. This may account for the statement in Mark that they didn't tell anyone, and for the statement in Luke that they "told this to the apostles; but these words seemed to them an idle tale, and they did not believe them" (24:11). Perhaps the strongest argument for the historicity of these accounts of the women at the tomb is that the stories fly in the face of established cultural behavior, and though the message was true, the women were not believed. Neither was the encounter of the women at the tomb referred to in the preaching of the earliest church—not by Paul in his letters nor by Peter in Acts. (I am aware that Paul's silence about the empty tomb is frequently cited as an argument on the other side, though the Pauline case for the re-creation is not incompatible with an empty tomb and may presuppose it.)[2] Thus, what reason could there be for keeping the narratives in the canonical Gospels except that the church believed the event to have really happened? In *The Founder of Christianity*, C. H. Dodd says, "It looks as if they [the evangelists] had on their hands a solid piece of tradition, which they were bound to respect because it came down to them from the first witnesses, though it did not add much cogency to the message they wished to convey, and they hardly knew what use to make of it."[3]

The women had encountered a message from God that Jesus lived. He was not to be found in the tomb but would be among his followers in Galilee as he had promised. According to Mark and Luke, they did not encounter their re-created Lord, but he would be known in Galilee. They heard the command to go and tell. Mark said that out of fear they did not spread the word. Luke said they did and were not believed. Matthew does not make it clear whether they were heard and believed. But I believe that the record that may have embarrassed the early church is clear. The first apostles and evangelists, against all cultural norms and probably against their own better judgment, were women—women named Mary and Salome and Joanna and others. They came to the tomb as they had remained near the cross,

2. See Jindrich Manek, "The Apostle Paul and the Empty Tomb," *Novum Testamentum* 2 (1956-57): 276-80. See also Ronald J. Sider, "The Pauline Conception of the Resurrection Body in I Cor. 15:35-54," *New Testament Studies* 21 (1974-75): 428-39; and Edward L. Bode, *The First Easter Morning: The Gospel Accounts of the Women's Visit to the Tomb of Jesus* (Rome: Biblical Institute Press, 1970), pp. 96-100.
3. Dodd, quoted in Robinson, *Can We Trust the New Testament?* p. 123.

unlike the men who had fled. Because it was true, the church preserved the traditions, though it did not know what to make of them.

The empty tomb is an embarrassment for many scholars because of their *a priori* assumptions about what God can and cannot do or what he would and would not do, or about what natural science does and does not allow. Of that I have spoken earlier. I agree with Wolfhart Pannenberg, who asks, "How could Jesus' disciples in Jerusalem have proclaimed his resurrection if they could be constantly refuted merely by viewing the grave in which his body was interred?"[4] Pannenberg quotes Paul Althaus: "The resurrection kerygma could not have been maintained in Jerusalem for a single day, for a single hour, if the emptiness of the tomb had not been established as a fact for all concerned."[5]

This is certainly on one end of the scholarly spectrum; however, it is interesting to note that a most cautious and careful New Testament scholar, Reginald Fuller, makes the following statement after treating the subject in considerable detail:

> Our investigations have shown at least that, contrary to widespread critical opinion, the empty tomb narrative with its angelophany rests on presuppositions which are not late Hellenistic and materialistic, but early Palestinian and apocalyptic. As such it is fully compatible with the kerygma of the resurrection as summarized in 1 Corinthians 15:4. Thus there is no reason why the pericope of the empty tomb should not be early and Palestinian in origin. . . . Beyond

4. Pannenberg, *Jesus—God and Man* (Philadelphia: Westminster Press, 1968), p. 100.
5. Althaus, quoted in Pannenberg, *Jesus—God and Man*, p. 100. William Lane Craig examines the Jewish polemic regarding the tomb—namely, that the guards were asleep or bribed, etc.—in Matt. 27:62-66 and 28:4, 11-14, and concludes that "the real value of Matthew's story is the incidental—and for that reason all the more reliable—information that Jewish polemic never denied that the tomb was empty but instead tried to explain it away. Thus the early opponents of the Christians themselves bear witness to the fact of the empty tomb" ("The Guard at the Tomb," *New Testament Studies* 30 [1984]: 279).

that the historian cannot go. We could only surmise that the basic nucleus was derived from a report given by Mary Magdalene to the disciples.[6]

However, Fuller concludes that "the disciples received Mary's report not as the origin and cause of their Easter faith, but as a vehicle for the proclamation of the Easter faith which they already held as a result of the appearances. It is as such that the Christian historian and community of faith can accept the report of the empty tomb today."[7]

I would agree that the postcrucifixion encounters between the disciples and their Lord, the appearances themselves, are the primary cause of the faith of the church community, not the news of the empty tomb. A moldering body in the tomb might invalidate their claim that they had seen the Lord; it certainly wouldn't help. But a tomb without a body does not demonstrate that Jesus lives. The account in Saint John's Gospel that the disciple who entered the tomb "saw and believed, for as yet they did not know the scripture, that he must rise from the dead" (20:8b-9) does not make much sense. It also conflicts significantly with the other narratives.[8]

The empty tomb points the way to faith, as the witness of the women most certainly did. It signals the end of the earthly Jesus and points to the re-creation that has come. It establishes women as the first witnesses, though the early Christians, caught as they were in an old and dying world, seemed not to know what to make of it.

Furthermore, the empty-tomb narratives may have functioned liturgically in the earliest church as pilgrims to

6. Fuller, *The Formation of the Resurrection Narratives*, pp. 69-70. See also Perkins, *Resurrection*, p. 94. After examining the arguments of Edward Bode and others, Perkins agrees with Fuller that the empty-tomb tradition is early.

7. Fuller, *The Formation of the Resurrection Narratives*, p. 70. See also Bode, *The First Easter Morning*, pp. 173-75.

8. Frans Neirynck argues that despite the differences between John's account and that in the Synoptics, the Johannine account does "depend" on the Synoptics ("John and the Synoptics— The Empty Tomb Stories," *New Testament Studies* 30 [1983-84]: 179).

Jerusalem congregated around a tomb believed to be that where Jesus was buried. Some scholars have speculated that this may explain the origin and use of the narratives;[9] if this is true, it would make them our earliest liturgical texts. Edward L. Bode, after very careful analysis, concludes that "the origin of Christian Sunday worship is to be found in the tradition of the visit to Jesus' tomb on the first day of the week." Bode is referring to the traditions lying behind the narratives of the empty tomb in the four Gospels. He bases his conclusion on "the use of Sunday for worship in the second half of the first century, the frequent celebration of the eucharist within the primitive communities and the insistence of the reliable tomb tradition upon a time during the first day of the week." He notes finally that "evidence of the tomb as the source of Sunday observance is superior to evidence that can be mustered in support of any other source for Sunday worship."[10] Others conclude that Sunday observance by the early Christians goes back to some of the appearance traditions, particularly those associated with a meal. (See pp. 65-67 herein.) Curiously, many liturgical churches, including the Episcopal Church, today follow a common lectionary that appoints the narrative of the empty tomb as the Gospel for the principal service on Easter Day. This follows a practice that goes back to the medieval church, which read the resurrection narratives in their entirety from all four Gospels during the octave of Easter, beginning at the vigil on the eve of Easter. Mark 16:1-8 was read on Easter Day.[11]

However, when all is said and done, the faith of the church is rooted not in the empty tomb but in the re-creation appearances of our Lord. At best the empty tomb is but a sign pointing to the appearances. To these we now turn.

9. See Jean Delorme, "The Resurrection and Jesus' Tomb: Mark 16,1-8 in the Gospel Tradition," in *The Resurrection and Modern Biblical Thought*, ed. P. DeSurgy (New York: Corpus Books, 1970), pp. 87-90. Edward L. Bode examines this speculation and rejects it (*The First Easter Morning*, pp. 130-32).

10. Bode, *The First Easter Morning*, p. 144.

11. Massey H. Shepherd, Jr., *The Oxford American Prayer Book Commentary* (New York: Oxford University Press, 1950), p. 164.

CHAPTER 4

The Appearance Narratives: Matthew 28:16-20; John 20:19-23; Luke 24:36-49

THE SEMINAL EXPERIENCE AND THE GROWTH OF THE TRADITION

Jesus re-created as Lord was known in the midst of his disciples soon after his crucifixion and death. This was the apostolic witness. They proclaimed "Jesus lives!" and "Jesus is Lord!" We have discussed Paul's witness to the Christ's appearance to himself and to others before him (1 Cor. 15:3-8). Passing on a tradition that he said he "received," he writes that Christ appeared "to the twelve" and "to all the apostles." We cannot be certain which of his followers constituted "the twelve" or "all the apostles." According to both Matthew (28:16) and Luke (24:33), there were only eleven after the betrayal by Judas. Furthermore, the term "apostles" is not used consistently by the evangelists or Paul.

Paul appears to be writing of two separate appearances to the inner group—one to "the twelve" and one to "all the apostles." However, it is possible that there was only one appearance of the Lord to the eleven assembled in one place and that all traditions of his appearance to the assembled group go back to a single event, which I will call the seminal experience. Alternatively, it is possible that there was more than one appearance to the eleven, but that one seminal appearance to the eleven, assembled in one place, lies behind the traditions that have given rise to the three concise narratives found in Matthew 28:16-20; John 20:19-23; and Luke 24:36-49.

In his commentary on John's Gospel, Raymond E. Brown examines the contradictions between and differences among the several appearance traditions and concludes that "the divergency as to locale and sequence found in the Gospel narratives of the post-resurrectional appearances of Jesus is not necessarily a refutation of the historicity of those appearances but may be the product of the way in which and the purpose for which the stories were told and preserved." After what he calls "highly speculative" reconstruction, Brown claims, "A more biblical approach is to suppose that one basic appearance underlies all the main Gospel accounts of the appearances to the Twelve (Eleven), no matter at what time or place the appearances are placed by the evangelists."[1]

The longer and more complex narratives of the appearances, such as Luke 24:13-35 and John 21, probably go back to separate oral traditions that may in turn go back to distinct appearances. But here we are concerned only with the three concise narratives of the appearance in the midst of the assembled "eleven" or "twelve."

How did these narratives come to be? (What follows is only informed conjecture.) The apostolic witnesses spoke of their encounters with Jesus. Words were not adequate to their experience; they knew that they spoke "foolishness" and "scandalously." They spoke of their encounters with the Re-created One from the point of view of witnesses who were powerfully moved and transformed by the encounter. They were not neutral observers but saw with the eyes of faith. The witnesses to his appearance to the eleven were few, and the Lord whom they met was one. Reports of the seminal experience should be unified by that fact, but the oral traditions that came out of the experience could have been colored by the humanity of the witnesses and by conventions of oral tradition.

L. W. Countryman in an article in *Second Century* at-

---

1. Brown, *The Gospel According to John XIII-XXI*, Anchor Bible, vol. 29A (Garden City, N.Y.: Doubleday, 1970), pp. 971-72.

tempts to account for the differences that occur in the three
versions of the *Regula Fidei* found in the writings of Tertullian at the end of the second and the beginning of the
third century; his work is relevant here. The three versions
are close in "pattern and content" but "far from identical."
However, says Countryman, if we consider the way in which
Tertullian uses them, we shall find that, "in every case, the
readers must be able to recognize the *regula* and must accept it as traditional and authoritative for Tertullian to
make his argument."[2] After examining the three works in
detail, Countryman concludes,

> In all three works, Tertullian's use of the *regula* reveals the
> following about the presuppositions of his readers: the *reg-
> ula* was an "old" authority well and widely known to them,
> both Catholics and Montanists; yet, it was an authority
> which they were prepared to recognize and accept in a vari-
> ety of versions, long and short, allowing considerable lati-
> tude in wording, but expecting a consistent and traditional
> pattern to emerge.[3]

Countryman asks how this variation in an authoritative tradition is possible. He suggests an "oral-social" theory. Briefly put, it posits that the *regula* was communicated orally in a
particular way by "composition in performance." This is a
term coined by students of oral poetry who have noted that
a performer reciting a particular epic "may claim to be repeating it word-for-word as he learned it; but . . . only the
general outline and content of the epic remain the same
from one performance to the next."[4] Applying this to the
regula, Countryman states,

> Tertullian's use of the *regula* suggests this kind of composi-
> tion in performance. Each time he recites the composition,
> he does so in a way influenced by his purpose and audience;

2. Countryman, "Tertullian and the Regula Fidei," *Second Century*
2 (1982): 211.
3. Countryman, "Tertullian and the Regula Fidei," p. 214.
4. Countryman, "Tertullian and the Regula Fidei," pp. 217-18.

yet, he does not feel that he is violating the "irreformable" nature of his material. This suggests that somehow both Tertullian and his audience have come to know the general and necessary structure of the *regula*—and also that they have some notion what embellishments and variations on it are acceptable and what would somehow constitute a given performance as a new and different composition.[5]

The social aspect of the theory relates to the needs and demands of the particular audience.[6]

If this interesting theory is applicable to the transmission of the *regula* in the latter part of the second and the early third century, then it might apply also to the transmission in the late first century of the three resurrection appearance narratives. They are, as we shall see, similar in pattern and general content, yet different in detail. They could go back to one encounter of the "eleven" or "twelve" (as suggested by Raymond Brown), be considered by those who repeated them and those who heard them to be authoritative, and yet vary in detail. Thus the usual argument against their historicity based on the differences between them might founder.

The oral traditions of his appearance probably circulated widely, and two generations separate the time of his postcrucifixion presence among the disciples and the time of the earliest written accounts of the appearances which we have. It was twenty-five years after these seminal events that Paul wrote the first letter to the Corinthians, forty years later that Mark wrote the empty-tomb narrative, and fifty to sixty years later that Matthew recorded the earliest narrative of the appearance.[7] This is about the length of time that separates us today from the presidency of Herbert Hoover. There might have been living witnesses in Matthew's day, and surely, by no stretch of the imagination, there were

---

5. Countryman, "Tertullian and the Regula Fidei," p. 217.
6. Countryman. "Tertullian and the Regula Fidei," pp. 217-18.
7. Throughout this book I have used the dates of Kumel and Wickenhauser-Schmid as listed in J. A. Fitzmyer's review article "Two Views of New Testament Interpretation," *Interpretation* 32 (1978): 310.

persons living then who had heard the oral traditions from the original witnesses.

Therefore, it is likely that traditions about the seminal encounters of the eleven with the Lord that circulated at the margin of the first and second century could have been corroborated or refuted by persons then living who heard them firsthand from the original witnesses. But most probably we don't have them in the precise language of the first witnesses, and if Countryman is right and the theory about the transmission of the *regula* applies, we should not expect consistency in detail but should anticipate a consistent pattern to emerge. It is likely that we have written traditions in the form in which a Christian community heard them read in worship,[8] influenced by the mind of an evangelist and the needs and use of the church of the late first century as they modified the "received" oral tradition. The text we have is a product of both early tradition and later editing (called "redaction"), but it was most likely used in a church where some individual could have compared it with what he or she had heard from the first witnesses. Thus I assume consistency of pattern and general content with the earlier traditions even though the narratives as written reflect the language and interest and practices of the late-first-century church as well as those of the evangelists themselves.

Another point is important to note. The church (let's call it "Matthew's church" or "Luke's church") knew the Lord as present to them. They experienced him in their midst. They would want to understand their experience of the Christ as present to them in the light of the seminal experience of the apostolic witnesses. They would naturally interpret one in the light of the other.

What we have, then, is the witness of the church on the brink of the second century to the seminal encounter of the apostolic witnesses as mediated through their own experience two generations later. The documents they produced

8. C. F. D. Moule, *The Birth of the New Testament*, rev. ed. (San Francisco: Harper & Row, 1982), p. 243.

are for us windows into the apostolic experience as well as paradigms for interpreting our experience of the Lord who is present.

The critic C. H. Dodd concludes that there were concise narratives of the type we have in Matthew 28:16-20 and John 20:19-21 "which, we have reason to suppose, represented most closely the corporate oral tradition of the primitive church."[9] Of these narratives he says,

> It appears, then, that the narratives in the gospels were not produced as expansion, by way of commentary or "midrash," of the list of appearances in the primitive tradition; while it is quite certain that the list was not compiled out of the gospels. We must conclude that the list of successive appearances on the one hand, as we have it in I Cor. xv.3-8, and as it is implied in Lk. xxiv. 33-4, and on the other hand the different types of narrative in the gospels, are independent of one another, and represent alternative methods of supplementing the simple statements of the *kerygma* in its baldest form, that Christ rose from the dead and that the apostles were witnesses to the fact, since he appeared to them after his Passion.[10]

Dodd may be read as implying that both the appearance narratives and the lists of appearances as "alternative methods of supplementing the simple statements of the *kerygma*" are the products of the creative imagination of the evangelists or possibly earlier originators of the traditions. I agree with his view of the independence of the appearance narratives, but I propose that they go back to oral traditions that in turn have their roots in the seminal event(s). Pheme Perkins in her study *Resurrection* agrees with Dodd that "the Kerygmatic proclamation of 1 Cor. 15:3-5 is not a summary of a resurrection narrative. Nor are the narratives simply imaginative expansion of the Kerygma." However, she

9. C. H. Dodd, "The Appearances of the Risen Christ: An Essay in Form-Criticism of the Gospels," in *More New Testament Studies* (Grand Rapids: Eerdmans, 1968), p. 127.

10. Dodd, "The Appearances of the Risen Christ," p. 127.

adds that "although it is generally agreed that the evangelists have used pregospel tradition in their accounts, the
nature of that tradition is hotly disputed." Dodd, she says,
"attempts to set up an inductive typology of the resurrection stories by asking what the common patterns in the
stories themselves are."[11] This is the course which I will
follow, though it will lead me further than Dodd and to
rather different conclusions than he reaches.

The conclusion of Matthew's Gospel (28:16-20) is the
earliest written narrative that we have of the appearance to
the disciples as a group, and is of the concise and unem-
bellished type about which Dodd writes. It compares in
form to the appearances recorded in John 20:19-23 and
Luke 24:36-49 to the assembled disciples. Taken together,
the three passages tell us a great deal about what I have
called the seminal experience and as paradigms can help us
better understand our own experience.

THE PATTERN IN THE APPEARANCE
NARRATIVES

I see a pattern in the three narratives of the appearances of
Jesus as Lord to the assembled disciples, a pattern that I
believe helps us to understand both the seminal experience
and our own. What follows is essentially an original contri-
bution, though it is influenced by the work of form critics
such as Dodd.[12] In describing this pattern I will speak of the

11. Perkins, *Resurrection: New Testament Witness and Contemporary Reflection* (Garden City, N.Y.: Doubleday, 1984), p. 114.

12. When this book was nearing completion, Pheme Perkins published her book *Resurrection*. In a footnote in that book I came across a
reference to a dissertation by Benjamin J. Hubbard published by the
Society of Biblical Literature and Scholars Press in 1974 entitled *The
Matthean Redaction of a Primitive Apostolic Commissioning: An Exegesis of
Matthew 28:16-20*. By using an inductive approach similar to mine and
also stimulated by C. H. Dodd, Hubbard has come up with an idea re-
markably similar to mine. He sees in the narrative of Matthew 28:16-20 a
pattern with *seven* elements that he calls Introduction, Confrontation,
Reaction, Commission, Protest, Reassurance, and Conclusion. He notes

encounter from the viewpoint of the disciple or witness. In my judgment it is the only viewpoint that is appropriate, as it is their experience to which they witness. It is their experience, furthermore, that is the paradigm for our experience. It does not make sense to tell the story from God's point of view.

The witnesses are, first, *aware of the presence* of Jesus who can be called Lord. When they identify the Present One with Jesus who was crucified they respond in awe and fear and by worshiping him, yet not without doubt. Second, they are *obedient to his command* to go and tell, to make disciples. They hear the Present One commanding them, and the response that is called forth is obedience. Third, they *trust in his promise*, a promise to be with them as they go forth in obedience, a promise of empowerment. The first two elements in the pattern are found in almost all of the narratives; the promise is found in several and is implied in others. This pattern is not the only one that can be seen, but it is one that makes the most sense of the material and that also makes the most sense out of our experience of new life in Christ.

My principle of interpretation is that the pattern should both be true to the biblical material in itself and function successfully as a paradigm for the Christian today. If and only if the biblical material can make sense out of contemporaneous life in Christ is it a living Word. We know that we are new creatures in Christ as we know Jesus to have been re-created. The appearance narratives are about the participation of the disciples in the new creation, and as we enter into their experience by an exercise of imagination,

---

parallels in John 20:19-23 and Luke 24:36-49 as well. Hubbard presents a careful case for the influence of Old Testament language associated with the call of Moses and the prophets, which I have noted also. He is interested primarily in analyzing the Matthew passage in the light of its antecedents in the tradition and does not consider the possibility of the pattern as a paradigm for Christian understanding today. While my book is an essay in hermeneutics, his book is an investigation into the process of redaction.

our experience of him is interpreted and enhanced. The process works both ways, of course. Our experience is useful in understanding theirs. The *pattern* that I see in the apostolic experience I see also in my own experience. The elements in the pattern—awareness of his presence, obedience to his command, and trust in his promise—are what I experience as faith. It is faith that is brought about by his presence, command, and promise and that involves my response in worship, obedience, and trust.

Now let us look in detail at the pattern in Matthew's narrative of the appearance to the eleven on the mountaintop. Then we will turn to John 20 and Luke 24 to see the manifestation of the pattern there. Table 1 shows the schematic form of each of the three narratives.

The Pattern in Matthew 28:16-20

Thousands of pages have been written about these five verses (the German scholar J. Lange wrote 573 pages).[13] An argument has raged over whether the resultant verses are principally tradition that Matthew inherited or largely the product of his pen or a combination of both. There is little agreement. The structure of the passage has also been much debated, with commentators seeing it as resembling an ancient enthronement hymn, a liturgical formula, or a royal decree. In an article in the *Journal of Biblical Literature* in 1977, John P. Meier reviewed the alternatives and concluded that "no form-critical category yet proposed fits Matthew 28:16-20." In his judgment the pericope is "*sui generis* . . . a product of Matthew's redactional activity—redactional activity, however, which worked upon some existing tradition."[14] Reginald Fuller sees verses 16-17 as

13. John P. Meier, "Two Disputed Questions in Matthew 28:16-20," *Journal of Biblical Literature* 96 (1977): 407. See also Gunther Bornkamm, "The Risen Lord and the Earthly Jesus—Mt. 28:16-20," in *The Future of Our Religious Past: Essays in Honor of Rudolf Bultmann*, trans. Charles E. Carlston, ed. James M. Robinson (New York: Harper & Row, 1971), pp. 203-8.

14. Meier, "Two Disputed Questions in Matthew 28:16-20," p. 424.

THE PATTERN IN MATTHEW, JOHN, & LUKE

	Matthew 28:16-20	John 20:19-23	Luke 24:36-49
SETTING	16 Now the eleven disciples went to Galilee, to the mountain to which Jesus had directed them.	19 On the evening of that day, the first day of the week, the doors being shut where the disciples were, for fear of the Jews,	33 And they found the eleven gathered together and those who were with them....
PRESENCE	(no description)	Jesus came and stood among them	36 As they were saying this, Jesus himself stood among them.
WORD		and said to them, "Peace be with you."	37 But they were startled and frightened, and supposed that they saw a spirit. 38 And he said to them, "Why are you troubled, and why do questionings rise in your hearts?"
SIGN		20 When he had said this, he showed them his hands and his side.	39 See my hands and my feet, that it is I myself...."
RESPONSE	17 And when they saw him they worshiped him; but some doubted.	Then the disciples were glad when they saw the Lord.	41 And while they still disbelieved for joy, and wondered....
COMMAND	18 And Jesus came and said to them, "All authority in heaven and earth has been given to me." 19 Go therefore and make disciples of all nations, baptizing them in the name of the Father and of the Son and of the Holy Spirit, 20 teaching them to observe all that I have commanded you;	21 Jesus said to them again, "Peace be with you." As the Father has sent me, even so I send you." 23 "If you forgive the sins of any, they are forgiven; if you retain the sins of any, they are retained."	44 Then he said to them, "These are my words which I spoke to you ... that everything written about me in the law of Moses and the prophets and the psalms must be fulfilled...." 47 "... and that repentance and forgiveness of sins should be preached in his name to all nations, beginning from Jerusalem." 48 You are witnesses of these things.
PROMISE	and lo, I am with you always, to the close of the age."	22 And when he had said this, he breathed on them, and said to them, "Receive the Holy Spirit."	49 And behold, I send the promise of my Father upon you; but stay in the city, until you are clothed with power from high."

something Matthew composed from early lists of appearances but not from a narrative, and verses 18-20 as a
fusion by Matthew of elements that were pre-Matthean.[15]

I do not think that the final verses of Matthew are a
received tradition passed on without alteration, nor that
they are purely a composition from Matthew's pen. Nor do
I believe that we must decide between the alternatives.
Whatever the accurate description of these verses, they
would not have passed muster in the church if they had not
been consistent and congruent with earlier tradition (for
reasons I have suggested earlier). Equally important, Matthew 28:16-20 displays the same pattern apparent in other
narratives of the appearance, and through that pattern
brings us into contact with the seminal experience and its
meaning for us.

With this very brief overview of a mountain of careful
work by the biblical critics, let us proceed to look at the
details of the passage under the rubrics of the pattern I
have established.

The Setting

The encounter is on a mountain in Galilee. The earliest
written tradition, the Markan story of the empty tomb, sets
us on the path to Galilee, but in John and elsewhere we
clearly have a Jerusalem appearance tradition as well. We
don't have to decide between Jerusalem and Galilee. It
seems reasonable that the disciples could have encountered
Jesus in either area or both. The mountain is more important than its location. In Matthew's tradition many of the
most important events in the drama have occurred on a
mountain: the temptation of Jesus by the devil (4:8), the
sermons on discipleship (5:1ff. and 8:1ff.), and the transfiguration (17:1-9). Every Jew and Christian knows that the
Law came to Moses on the mountain; so does that discipleship that succeeded the Law. The mountain is where

---

15. Fuller, *The Formation of the Resurrection Narratives* (New York: Macmillan, 1971), pp. 82, 92. See also Perkins, *Resurrection*, pp. 131-32, for a
discussion of redaction versus tradition.

God meets man. What is more appropriate as a place where
the new creation is set forth? (Is Luke giving us another
version of this same tradition in the ascension narrative?)
Herman C. Waetjen in *The Origin and Destiny of Humanness*
sees the mountain as the *axis mundi*, the mountain of the
sovereignty of God and his Son.[16]

The Presence

What is most noticeable is that so little is said about the
presence; there is no apocalyptic language, no description
at all. It is what Robert H. Smith in *The Easter Gospels* calls a
"marvel of reserve."[17] As we will see, this terse simplicity is
what typifies what Dodd calls the "concise" appearance narratives. The narrator merely tells us that Jesus came or
notes that he was there.

The response of the disciples is what claims our attention: "and when they saw him they worshiped him; but
some doubted" (v. 17). We will look at three words: "saw,"
"worshiped," and "doubted."

The Greek word for "saw" *(idontes)* is better translated
"having seen." It gives us no information about who was
seen or how he was seen. Furthermore, we get few clues
from Matthew's usage elsewhere. In 14:26 the disciples
"see" Jesus (same verb) walking on the water, and they ex-
claim, "It is a ghost!" This is extraordinary or at least ambiguous "seeing," as in this narrative. (See the later discussion
of the response of the disciples to Christ's presence.) In the
earlier narrative of the women at the tomb, the angel says to
the women, "Come, see (same verb) the place where he lay"
(28:6). Though angelic visitors are certainly extraordinary,
a form of the verb *oraō* is used here in a direct or common
way.

Can we get clues from outside the Book of Matthew
about the kinds of verbs the first-century church used to

16. Waetjen, *The Origin and Destiny of Humanness* (San Rafael, Cal.:
Omega Books, 1976), p. 254.
17. Smith, *The Easter Gospels: The Resurrection of Jesus According to the
Four Evangelists* (Minneapolis: Augsburg, 1983), p. 78.

describe the appearance? As we have noted, Paul uses the same verb—*oraō*—in passing on the tradition that he "received" (1 Cor. 15:3-8). It can be translated as "was seen" or "appeared" or something like "caused himself to be seen by." Most important, Paul also uses it in describing his own encounter with Jesus on the road to Damascus: "he appeared also to me." If we interpret Matthew's use of *idontes* in the light of Paul's use of *ōphthē,* then "saw" involves visual perception, not insight or second sight.

Many Christians may be comfortable with the physical appearances in Luke and John, others with the "bright light" of Paul. Paul, as we have noted, makes no distinction between the appearance to him and those earlier appearances to the others that he lists. In any event, Matthew, like Paul, is referring to perceiving and responding to someone present outside of and apart from himself. What is most important is that the disciples identified Jesus as Lord. Someone was present among them, to them, in their midst, someone whom they identified with Jesus who was crucified. They "knew" in the deepest sense of that word that Jesus was present. That is absolutely clear in all the versions. It was the Jesus of the cross who was with them. Despite crucifixion and death, Jesus was present. At minimum the details of the prints of the nails in John's account are included to make that point. The One who was present was in continuity with the person of Jesus, who had made them disciples and taught them and died for them. However "seeing" is construed, it must include "seeing that" Jesus was present.

He is not only present, but present as Lord, for "they worshiped him." The Greek word literally means "fell on their faces." This is Matthew's word; he uses it thirteen times compared with the two times Mark and Luke each use it. Matthew uses this word here, as well as in his recounting of the worship of the infant Jesus by the Magi (chap. 2) and his recording of the reaction of the disciples to Jesus after they have seen him walking on the water (14:33). Jesus who is present is clearly also Lord, and as Lord he calls forth "worship." The Magi saw his lordship at birth, and the disciples see it on the mountaintop. They respond in worship. (Luke in the story of the Emmaus road will tell us more about the presence in worship.)

"But some doubted." For us these are perhaps the most important words in the appearance narratives because they leave room for us to doubt. He who is present is not so clearly and evidently Jesus and Lord that he *necessitates* worship. There is room for doubt that Jesus is Lord, that the Present One can be identified with Jesus of the cross. Some of the eleven doubted, some who, after all, had the advantage over us of having been with him in the flesh. There is certainly doubt present in the other appearance narratives as well—in both Luke 24 and John 20. The story of Thomas comes immediately to mind. The word Matthew uses—in Greek, *distazō*—is used in no other book in the New Testament and is not used in the Septuagint.[18] It indicates uncertainty or the inability to make up one's mind on the basis of the evidence—not unbelief or simply perplexity.[19] Matthew uses it one other time in the story of Peter's attempt to come to Jesus over the water—the only other event where the disciples respond to Jesus by worshiping him (14:28-33). Matthew's use of the same word in the earlier passage, where it is translated as "doubt," may help us to understand his use here. Peter has cried out, "Lord, if it is you, bid me come to you on the water." Peter is told to "come," but when he sees the wind, he is afraid and begins to sink. When he cries out, "Lord, save me," Jesus reaches out his hand and says to Peter, "O man of little faith, why did you doubt?" (14:28-31). Peter expresses doubt at the beginning of this exchange ("Lord, if it is you . . ."). The doubt could be either over a question of identity (is Jesus really Lord) or power (does he have the power to save). Doubt in the appearance narrative appears to relate to the

18. I. P. Ellis, "But Some Doubted," *New Testament Studies* 14 (1967-68): 575.

19. Ellis, "But Some Doubted," pp. 576-67.

identity of the Present One. Is the Lord present, and is Jesus the Lord?

The evidence, whatever it was, did not overwhelm the minds and hearts of the disciples. They were free to worship or to doubt. Jesus who was present as Lord did not take the disciples by storm. Even so with us. Physical proof adequate for empirical scientific judgments is not offered. And even if it was offered, decisions based on it are not especially blessed. Jesus asks Thomas, "Have you believed because you have seen me? Blessed are those who have not seen and yet believe" (John 20:29). Seeing is not necessarily believing. There is room for the doubting and uncertain disciple.

Doubt that it is Jesus who is present as Lord is not dispelled in the Matthew narrative by physical proof as perhaps it is in the other appearance narratives. The Lord's presence remains ambiguous, and therefore we too are free to doubt. If doubt is dispelled at all, it is dispelled in the process of the disciples' carrying out the command and in the disciples' experience of the continuing presence of the Lord. Matthew does not tell us. Perhaps he did not know what to do with the doubting disciples in the received tradition. However, doubt is not his major concern. It is discipleship. Action, not assent, is what is called for. The fact that Matthew does not comment on the doubt nor attempt to resolve it points, in my judgment, to the historical roots of the narrative. I believe the appearance tradition included the disciples' responding to Christ with doubt mixed with worship, and the three evangelists record it, although each handles it differently.

The Command

Nevertheless, Matthew's emphasis in describing the response to the presence of the Lord identified as Jesus is not on seeing but hearing. His presence is indicated primarily by what is heard, not by what is seen. The auditory elements, the command and the promise, are emphasized, almost to the exclusion of the visual.

The command to the disciples and to us proceeds out of

the authority of the Son. "All authority in heaven and on earth has been given (or 'delivered') to me" (Matt. 28:18b). The authority delivered by the Father to the Son is total (see also Matt. 11:27): it extends to the outer edges of the universe, to all nations, and to the end of time. He who is present has the full authority of the Father. Because his authority extends to heaven and earth, his disciples are to go to all nations. His command is tied to his authority by the word "therefore" *(oun)*.

It should be remembered that the command issues forth from his person, from the One who is present. There is no command without the presence of Jesus who is Lord. In part, this is what the statement of authority is about. His authoritative person is the source of the command and of the disciples' response, and it is the reason for the disciples' obedience and for our obedience. Otherwise, we are dealing with pure moralism or pure spiritualism. The ethical dimension or element presupposes the personal presence and is conditioned by it.

The command is threefold (28:19-20a). Those who know him as present and hear his voice are to make disciples, to baptize, and to teach. To do this, they must go forth. They are not called upon to remain on the mountaintop, basking in the presence of the Lord (a constant temptation of the church in all times, whether sacramentalist or pietist). They must go. Though the Greek *(poreuthentes)* is an auxiliary form that means "going" ("Hurry up and get going to make disciples"),[20] "to go" is central to the command in most of the appearance narratives—"Go and tell." This is also the case in the appearance of God to Moses and the prophets: he commands, "Go to your kindred," "Go to your people," "Go to Pharaoh," and so forth. Disciples are those on the move. They are not to stay on the mountain or in the sanctuary—a lesson that has to be relearned in every generation.

They are to bring others into discipleship, not only Jews

20. Smith, *The Easter Gospels,* p. 82.

but all nations. The Greek word translated "nations" *(ethnē)* is the root of our word "ethnic" and suggests strongly that the church is called to reach beyond its ethnic ghettos. It could in Matthew's usage be limited to the contrast between Jews and Gentiles, but in either case it represents a calling to mission beyond the Jews alone.

Being a disciple involves baptism (bringing people into the community of the disciples). While the form of the command in John and Luke does not explicitly involve baptism, Reginald Fuller points out that the command in the narratives of the other evangelists does include the forgiveness of sins, which implicitly involves baptism.[21] The Trinitarian formula may be rather late in time, but late or not, baptism in the name of the Trinity is the form and the sign by which disciples make other disciples, and has been for most of Christian history.

Being a disciple not only involves bringing in new disciples by baptism; it also involves teaching. A disciple is a learner. Before the crucifixion Jesus was the Teacher, and his followers were learners or disciples. Now they are also teachers. He remains the source of all teaching, but the disciple becomes a teacher-learner. The teaching involves "all that I have commanded you" (v. 20a). In this one phrase, the command has embraced the teaching of Jesus' entire ministry, both in word and act. This command has Old Testament roots, as the people Israel were called to observe all the commandments of God. The distinction is that the disciples (and we) are to observe what *Jesus* has commanded. (In the Sermon on the Mount in Matt. 5:21-48, note the distinction between what men of old say and what "*I* say unto you.")

In *Resurrection* Pheme Perkins points out, "The three commands that make up the commission to the disciples remove limitations that had existed during the ministry of Jesus. The limitation to Israel (Mt. 10:5-6; 15:24) is replaced by the mission to 'all the peoples.' Circumcision as

---

21. Fuller, *The Formation of the Resurrection Narratives*, p. 86.

the sign of belonging is replaced by baptism. The Torah is replaced by what Jesus had taught."[22]

The command that is heard by the disciples on the mount, by the church of Matthew, and by us issues forth from the authority of the Son, authority that reaches to heaven and earth, to all peoples, and to the end of time. They and we are commanded to make disciples, and this involves going out teaching and baptizing in his name. No longer is such a command limited to the lonely prophet. Jeremiah was called to go to whatever people God sent him to and to say whatever he was told to say. He was also promised that God would be with him and keep him safe (Jer. 1:7-8). We are now called to obey a similar command by the One who calls us his disciples and his brothers and sisters (Matt. 28:10). Only in the new creation are his followers "brethren." The word is not used in Matthew prior to the death and re-creation. In John's Gospel Jesus calls his disciples "friends" (15:14-15) and "brethren" (20:17).

The Promise

Those who know him as present and go forth in his name in obedience to his command do so trusting in his promise: "And lo (or 'behold'), I am with you always, to the close of the age" (v. 20b). Moses had heard the promise that God would be with him (Exod. 3:12), and Jeremiah that God would be with him and keep him safe (Jer. 1:8). We hear that God will go with us as we go about making disciples, baptizing and teaching. Matthew has prepared us for this, for the name of Jesus is "Emmanuel," which Matthew takes pains to explain means "God with us" (1:23). This is the very name of God himself, and this too has Old Testament roots. When Moses asks God what his name is (Exod. 3:13), God's answer is usually translated as "I am who I am," and Moses is told to tell the people "I am" has sent him. God's name in this translation is "I AM." Martin Buber in his book *Moses* has made an interesting suggestion that the name of God is

22. Perkins, *Resurrection*, pp. 133-34.

mis-translated in the Septuagint as "I AM" and is better translated as "I shall be present." He also suggests that *ehyeh asher ehyeh* (Exod. 3:14), usually translated as "I am who I am," is better translated as "I shall be present that I shall be present."[23] Indeed, God promised Moses that he would be present with him (Exod. 3:12) and that he would be present with Moses' mouth (Exod. 4:12). There is obviously a verbal connection between the *egō eimi* of Matthew 28:20b and the Septuagint translation of *ehyeh asher ehyeh (egō eimi ho ōn)*. For Moses, God is the Present One; for the disciples and for us, it is Jesus as Lord. The promise to Moses is similar to the promise that the disciples are asked to trust (Matt. 28:20b) and we also who have learned from them.

He is present to us as and when the Present One is known to be Jesus of the ministry and the cross. We know him, furthermore, as we go forth to make disciples in his name, bringing them into the family of his brethren by baptism and teaching them what we have learned from him. Bruce J. Malina, in an article in *New Testament Studies*, analyzes the language about presence and promise thus: "The presence of Jesus is experienced and thus known only in the process of carrying out the decree to make all nations disciples."[24] The Lord Jesus does not ask us to remain with him on the mountain but tells us to go forth with him to the corners of the earth and to all peoples. We don't go alone; we go forth with many brethren and with him. Trusting in his promise, we can go forth in his name, the name that is "God with us" or "I am present."

Matthew has prepared us for this expectation earlier in his Gospel, where we have also the promise of Jesus that "where two or three are gathered in my name, there am I *(eimi)* in the midst of them" (18:20). Furthermore, we expect to find Jesus as Christ present when we minister to the least of his brethren (Matt. 25:40). The promise in which

23. Buber, *Moses* (Oxford: East & West Library, 1946), pp. 46-55.
24. Malina, "The Literary Structure and Form of Matt. 28:16-20," *New Testament Studies* 17 (1970-71): 103.

the disciples trust and in which the church of Matthew trusts and in which we trust is that Jesus will be present when we are assembled in his name and when we go out in his name, making disciples, teaching, baptizing, and caring for the least of his brethren. This promise extends to the edge of the earth and to the end of time. Hearing this promise, we have the courage to take seriously his command, for it is only in the trust of that promise that we are bold enough to go forth in his name as both learners and friends.

The Pattern in John 20:19-23

John's Gospel, as we have it, may have been written or edited in the generation following that from which Matthew's Gospel comes, perhaps sixty to seventy years after the crucifixion. Not only is it later, it is quite independent of the Synoptic Gospels. Nevertheless, scholars such as Reginald Fuller and Raymond Brown believe that John may have relied on traditions of the Easter appearances that were also known to other evangelists, particularly Luke. But he seemed to have had access to traditions unknown to them as well.[25]

Nevertheless, despite the difference in the time of writing and despite the apparent independence of traditions, the same pattern that I have observed at the close of Matthew's Gospel is clearly discernible in the terse account of the appearance of the Christ to the disciples narrated in John 20:19-23. I should hasten to add that I am not saying that the pattern I see reflects the intention of the evangelist. Rather, I am suggesting that the seminal encounter with the Lord has a structure in itself and is discernible at least in the three brief narratives of the appearance of the Lord in the midst of the eleven. It is there despite the obvious differences in the perspectives and language of the evange-

25. Fuller, *The Formation of the Resurrection Narratives*, pp. 131-32; and Brown, *The Gospel According to John*, pp. 1018ff.

lists. Oral traditions bearing this pattern or structure could have been transmitted by the process discussed at the beginning of this chapter. However transmitted, the pattern is there.

Table 1 shows the threefold pattern in John 20:19-23 compared with Matthew 28:16-20 and also with Luke 24:36-49. The latter has much in common with John. In fact, Reginald Fuller has concluded that the Lukan and Johannine narratives go back to a common oral tradition.[26] (The Lukan story of the appearance to the eleven will be discussed in the next section.)

The Setting

The encounter in the closed room is set in Jerusalem and follows in the Gospel immediately after the discovery of the empty tomb, first by Mary Magdalene and then by Peter and the Beloved Disciple. We are told by the evangelist, "Then the other disciple (John, by tradition), who reached the tomb first, also went in, and he saw and believed; for as yet they did not know the scripture, that he must rise from the dead" (20:8-9). Of the three—Mary, Peter, and the Beloved Disciple—only the latter "believes" solely on the basis of the empty tomb. Then Mary encounters Jesus, and though she mistakes him for the gardener, she finally recognizes him and goes to the disciples saying, "I have seen the Lord" (v. 18).

Mary Magdalene has told the disciples that she has seen the Lord. Peter and the Beloved Disciple have seen the tomb empty, and at least the latter believes on the basis of that experience alone. Then comes the meeting in the closed room. There is no mention of the prior news. The disciples are behind closed doors for "fear of the Jews." There is no expectation of the Lord's coming and no immediate response to his presence as is described in Matthew's narrative. Jesus shows them the proof of his wounds before their joy is apparent. This seems odd in the light of John

20:1-18. This may point to a narrative of the appearance to the eleven that is quite independent of the previous narrative in the earlier part of the chapter; Raymond Brown believes so.[27] The evangelist may not have wished to force the earlier traditions to conform with one another. In any event, the setting is one of fearful disciples hiding behind closed doors in Jerusalem, not obviously expectant of the coming of the Lord.

The Presence

As in the case of Matthew's narrative, the details are sparse. John 20:19—"Jesus came and stood among them (literally 'in the midst')"—uses language reminiscent of Matthew 18:20: "Where two or three are gathered in my name, there am I in the midst of them." Possibly we are meant to conclude that he came through a closed door. We are in a different narrative world from Matthew, for here physical proof of his identity is offered. Jesus speaks a greeting that could be the ordinary Jewish greeting or the one used at special moments of revelation, "Peace be with you." Earlier he has promised (according to John), "Peace I leave with you; my peace I give to you" (14:27), and he has prayed that "in me you may have peace" (16:33). Thus the greeting of peace may provide a special word of recognition for the disciples.

If there is ambiguity about the greeting, there is less about the wounds. Jesus shows his hands and his side, and "*then* the disciples were glad when they saw the Lord" (v. 20, RSV); "*Therefore* the disciples rejoiced, having seen the Lord" (v. 20). By word and sign of the cross they identified the One who was present with Jesus who was crucified. There are no such signs in Matthew, but such signs should not be needed for faith. There is no mention of doubt as there is in Matthew's account. However, one who was not present—Thomas— later demands a physical sign similar to that which was given to the rest of the disciples.

27. Brown, *The Gospel According to John XIII-XXI*, pp. 1027-28.

What are we to make of the nature of the evidence apparently needed for recognition according to the evangelist
John? Many biblical critics see the showing of the wounds as
part of a tendency over time for the stories to place more
emphasis on the corporeal, from the chaste version in Matthew, to the Re-created One's eating with the disciples in
Luke's account and in the appendix of John 21, to the un-
canonical "Gospels," which are even more literal. On the
other hand, if Jesus came through a closed door, the body is
hardly physical. The nature of his presence is ambiguous
here, as in Matthew. In any event, it is clear that the author
of this Gospel does not believe that seeing and touching the
wound are necessary for faith, and that is the point of the
story about Thomas.

The disciples' response to the presence of the Lord is
rejoicing—not worship mixed with doubt, as in Matthew, or
joy mixed with disbelief and wonder, as in Luke.

The Command

A command is central to the encounter experience, as we
have seen in the Matthew story. Here the Re-created One
says, "As the Father has sent me, even so I send you" (v. 21).
The disciples are to be apostles, those who are sent. The Son
has been sent, and his followers are sent forth likewise.
There is no explicit universal mission, as in Matthew; we are
not told to whom they are sent. However, we know from the
discourse on the Good Shepherd in John that he has "other
sheep, that are not of this fold" whom he must bring in "so
there shall be one flock, one shepherd" (10:16); and in the
high priestly prayer (17:20-21) Jesus prays for those "who
(are to) believe in me through their word (that of the disciples or those who are sent forth)." There is no specific mention of teaching or baptism, as there is in Matthew.
However, they are empowered to forgive sins, which, of
course, is closely associated with baptism. The disciples are
told, "If you forgive the sins of any, they are forgiven; if you
retain the sins of any, they are retained" (v. 23). Forgiveness of sins is necessary to enter into the new creation. In

part this is what the baptism of John the Baptist prepares
for. To enter into the new, one must break the power of the
old, and forgiveness is the key.

The disciples had committed apostasy. As the crucifixion
had approached, they had forsaken Jesus and fled. By
coming among them after his death, he restores their fellowship with him and their fellowship with one another. His
presence rebuilds the community, and forgiveness is the
door through which they pass into the new creation. Forgiven, they are to be agents for the forgiveness of others
and through forgiveness to bring others into fellowship
with them and with Jesus, who they now know as Lord.
Forgiven and carrying out his command, they are no longer
"servants" but "friends": "You are my friends if you do
what I command you. No longer do I call you servants"
(John 15:14-15). Forgiveness extends the fellowship of
friends. Though baptism is not mentioned as it is in Matthew, baptism is the event that recognizes the new status of
the forgiven.

The command, though less detailed and without Matthew's preoccupation with discipleship, is nonetheless a
mission command, a command to go forth. In obedience to
his command, they and we do serve him, but as friends, as
brothers and sisters.

The Promise

Those who share in the joy of his presence in their midst,
those who respond to his command to go out as he has gone
out, receive a promise. As he had promised earlier, they will
not be orphaned (14:18); he will come to them. Now he
breathes on them, saying, "Receive the Holy Spirit" (20:22).
The promise has been spelled out in the body of the Gospel,
where the disciples are told that it is necessary that he go
away in order that the Holy Spirit will come to them (16:7).
From the discussion in John 14:25-31 we know that the
Spirit is sent in his name and that the Spirit "will teach you
all things, and bring to your remembrance all that I have
said to you" (v. 26). In this same passage Jesus reminds the

disciples that he will come to them (v. 28) and that his peace
he will leave with them (v. 27). The Spirit, therefore, is the
mode of Jesus' continuing presence with them, and the
promise is not unlike that of Matthew (28:20).

In the disciples' final encounter with Jesus, this promise
is enacted in a startling way unique in the Gospel narratives.
Jesus infuses them with God's spirit by breathing upon
them. A Jew, hearing this account, could hardly miss the
point. God created humankind by breathing life into Adam
(Gen. 2:7), and here we have a new act of creation. A new
humanity is being created, with the firstborn, Jesus the
Christ, imparting the spirit so that his followers may have
life and, like him, may become a "life-giving spirit" (1 Cor.
15:45). He is, according to John, "the resurrection and the
life" (11:25). Those who believe in him will have life (11:26).
He has come that we "may have life, and have it abun-
dantly" (10:10). He, the Re-created One, is by his breath
giving life to a new humanity. The promise, according to
John, is nothing short of an infusion of the spirit, first into
the apostles and through them into the church.

The presence, the command, and the promise are all
prominent, and, as in the Matthew narrative, there is also a
commentary on the response of the church. In Matthew it is
limited to the doubt among those who responded to Christ's
presence by worshiping him. In John's Gospel we have a
unique narrative about doubt and faith.

Doubting Thomas and Faith

The origins of the story about Thomas are not clear.
Reginald Fuller says, "Recent criticism seems to be generally agreed that the Thomas story is not a free creation of
the Evangelist."[28] Raymond Brown comes to the opposite
conclusion: "The Thomas story . . . has been created by the
evangelist who has taken and dramatized a theme of doubt
that originally appeared in the narrative of the appearance

28. Fuller, *The Formation of the Resurrection Narratives*, p. 142.

to the disciples."[29] In either case, the story provides a counterpoint to the physical evidence that appears to have preceded the *recognition* of the Lord by the disciples in the pericope just discussed.

The other disciples tell Thomas, "We have seen the Lord," the same message that they were given by Mary Magdalene. Thomas insists that he "will not believe" unless he sees "in his hands the print of the nails, and place my finger in the mark of the nails" (v. 25). He must see and touch to believe. But as we know, when the offer is made and he is asked to be "believing," not "faithless," he confesses "My Lord and my God!" He has seen but not touched. The Lord asks, "Have you believed because you have seen me?" (v. 29). Of course, in this narrative Thomas has seen, and this is true of the other disciples as well. Only the Beloved Disciple at the empty tomb believed without seeing. For the apostles, the first witnesses, seeing is believing. This is apparently John the evangelist's belief about the apostolic witnesses. In the world of Matthew and Paul, identity of Jesus as Lord does not require corporeal proof, though there may be some. Furthermore, it is possible to be in the presence of the re-created Jesus and not necessarily know who is present.

But—and the "but" is crucial—the last utterance of the Christ in John 20, which is addressed to all who would come after, is this: "Blessed are those who have not seen and yet believe" (v. 29). We cannot see him in any literal sense of the word, yet we are blessed. Thomas is not condemned for wanting physical proof, but we are blessed for not demanding or requiring it. In both Matthew and John, seeing is not necessarily believing. The encounters are not absolutely compelling; there is room for human freedom and doubt. And the blessed are those who don't require proof for faith. What is required is a spirit that is open to the word of peace, and that sees that the cross defines the Lordly presence (the

29. Brown, *The Gospel According to John XIII-XXI*, p. 1031.

true meaning of the print of the nails). What is required is a person who feels the breath of the empowering spirit propelling him or her to go forth in the Lord's name as his friend with a word of forgiveness. This is "seeing" without seeing.

John modifies the increasing literalization of the appearance stories with his final beatitude. We have not left the world of Matthew entirely for the world of Luke. We are in a world where the new creation comes as an offer to humanity created free to reject it, free to be skeptical, and free to doubt; yet where freedom, if exercised in rejection of Jesus as Lord, forecloses forgiveness of sins.

The Pattern in Luke 24:36-49

Luke's Gospel appears to have been written around the same time as Matthew and perhaps ten years earlier than John, fifty to sixty years or two generations removed from the events of Easter as described. The portion of the narrative on which we are focusing our attention has, in the opinion of many commentators, a great deal in common with John 20:19-23, even though it may have been written earlier.[30] I am discussing it after John 20:19-23 because it is more embellished. The two passages appear to look back to a single earlier tradition, one that differs from Matthew. A look at Table 1 will demonstrate this. There are many verbal similarities: Jesus "stood among them"; he showed them his hands and his feet (Luke) or his side (John); they respond with joy *(charas);* their mission involves forgiveness of sins; and they are to receive the Holy Spirit (in Luke, be "clothed with power from on high"). Both Luke and John are much more embellished narratives with a stronger corporeal emphasis than the spare appearance narrative of Matthew. Luke goes further than John in material detail

30. Perkins, *Resurrection,* p. 163. See also A. R. C. Leaney, "The Resurrection Narratives in Luke 24:12-53," *New Testament Studies* 2 (1955-56): 110-14.

and is without the Thomas narrative and its beatitude to mitigate the material emphasis.

Despite the differences in detail, the pattern is clearly present in this Lukan narrative.

The Setting

Earlier in the chapter (24:1-11), Mary Magdalene and the other women visited the tomb, found it empty, and heard the good news of Christ's entrance into new life: "Why do you seek the living among the dead?" (v. 5). They returned from the tomb and told what they had seen and heard "to the eleven and to all the rest" (v. 9). Their audience, also described as "the apostles," "did not believe them"; the words of the women "seemed to them an idle tale ('folly' or 'humbug')" (v. 11). Then the Lukan narrative continues with the story of the two disciples on the road to Emmaus (discussed separately below). These two returned to Jerusalem, where "they found the eleven gathered together and those who were with them" (v. 33). The Emmaus disciples are told, "The Lord has risen indeed, and has appeared to Simon!" (v. 34). There is no account of the appearance to Simon.

The Presence

The Lukan narrative continues: "As they were saying this, Jesus himself stood among them (literally 'in the midst of them')" (v. 36). The group includes not just the eleven but "those who were with them" and the recent addition of the two who had walked the Emmaus road. Assuming Peter to be there, at least three of them have seen the Lord, and all of them have heard about his appearance. In the light of this, the next few verses are surprising. "But they were startled and frightened, and supposed that they saw a spirit (*pneuma*)" (v. 37). Though three of them are prepared for his coming by their own experience and the rest by the testimony of others, they are terrified. His identity is not obvious, nor does it compel them to recognize him.

He asks why they are troubled, and he proceeds to show

them the marks of the cross and to bid them to "handle me, and see; for a spirit has not flesh and bones as you see that I have" (v. 40). This is a long way from Matthew and from the spiritual body of Saint Paul, who wrote to the Corinthians, "Flesh and blood cannot inherit the kingdom of God, nor does the perishable inherit the imperishable" (1 Cor. 15:50).

The assembled disciples respond with a mixture of emotions: "And while they still disbelieved for joy, and wondered. . . " (v. 41). The passage is literally "And yet disbelieving them from the joy and marveling." Though a bit confused, it is clear enough that joy and wonder are mixed with disbelief, not too far off from the mixture of "worship" and "doubt" of Matthew. But Luke goes further, for "while they still disbelieved for joy" the Present One asks for something to eat and takes it and eats it "before them" (v. 43). We can't be certain about what Luke is doing, but he may be "fighting docetic, gnostic, or spiritualizing misinterpretations, as Paul also did on Hellenistic soil."[31] We are left with a great gulf between Paul and Matthew and Mark on the one hand and the corporeal emphasis of the Lukan narrative on the other. I don't think the disparate portrayals of the re-created Jesus known as the Christ can be harmonized. Luke can be rationalized but can hardly be taken literally if Paul is to be taken seriously.

The pattern, despite the divergence of detail, is still apparent. Jesus appears; he is present, and yet initially it is not clear who he is. The marks of the cross are revealed, and then he is identified. The disciples know that Jesus is Lord and respond with wonder and joy mixed with disbelief.

The Command

The form of the command is not as obvious as that in Matthew and John, but it is there nonetheless. The disciples, whom Luke also calls "apostles," are to be "witnesses of these things" (v. 48). Their witness involves preaching "in his name to all nations" (v. 47). What are all these things to

31. Smith, *The Easter Gospels*, p. 123.

which they are to bear witness? (The Greek word translated "witness" is *martures,* from which we derive "martyr.") They are to proclaim and bear witness to "my words which I spoke to you, while I was still with you, that everything written about me in the law of Moses and the prophets and the psalms must be fulfilled" (v. 44). This is not too far from Matthew 28:19-20, where the Lord commands them to "make disciples of all nations, . . . teaching them to observe all that I have commanded you." In both cases the teaching or proclamation is to be "to all nations." The disciples are to proclaim *his* words that he spoke to them and "all that *I* commanded you." Both center on the teaching of Jesus himself. Luke goes further, including everything in the law and the prophets and the psalms—in other words, everything in Scripture written about him must be fulfilled. As the disciples hear the command, their minds are "opened" to "understand the scriptures" (v. 45). Hearing and obeying the command involves being opened to the meaning of Scripture, particularly as it reveals Christ present in it. (See pp. 61-63 herein.)

They are given a synopsis, the heart of the proclamation to which they are to bear witness: "Thus it is written, that the Christ should suffer and on the third day rise from the dead" (v. 46). He is the interpreter of the word of God, and he is the message.

This preaching to all the nations also involves proclaiming "repentance and forgiveness of sins" (v. 47). This is integral to the command in John and in Matthew instructing the disciples to baptize, which, as we know, is a baptism of repentance for the remission or forgiveness of sins. Matthew speaks of disciples and teachers, John of those who are sent (apostles), Luke of witnesses and preachers. All are ways of speaking of those who go forth in obedience to the command of the Lord.

The Promise

The witnesses to all nations to his presence and his words are sent forth with a promise: "And behold, I send the promise of my Father upon you; but stay in the city, until you are clothed with power from on high" (v. 49). The promise of the Father that involves being "clothed with power from on high" is obviously the gift of the Holy Spirit. In Matthew the Lord promises his presence with them, for he is Emmanuel. In John he breathes on them and gives them the Holy Spirit. According to Luke he sends— literally "sends forth"—the promise of the Father. In all three cases the Re-created One, Jesus as Lord, is the active agent: he is to be with them; he breathes the spirit upon them; he sends forth the promise of the Father.

The witnesses (Luke) or teacher-learners (Matthew) go forth as brethren (Matthew) or friends (John) in the power of the promise of the presence (Matthew) or the spirit (John) or the promise of the power from on high (Luke). In all three traditions they share in the power of the Lord whom they have encountered, sharing his authority to teach (Matthew) and his power to forgive (Luke and John). But this empowerment is modified by all that he has said and demonstrated about servanthood. Brothers and friends are not masters; neither are disciples or learners masters. This empowerment that comes from his spiritual presence creates not a new authoritarian hierarchy (as the old world has) but a new society in which power is exercised not over subjects but among friends and brethren.

CHAPTER 5

He Was Known to Them in the Breaking of the Bread

LUKE 24:13-35

In the three brief narratives of the appearance of the Lord Jesus among his disciples (Matt. 28:16-20; John 20:19-23; Luke 24:36-49), we have seen a pattern common to all three. Jesus is present as Lord, he commands them to go forth in his name, and he promises to be with them in spirit. Though doubting, the disciples were joyful, and, as we know from their witness, they obeyed his command, going forth into the world trusting in his promise.

The pattern discernible in the concise narratives of the appearance to the assembled disciples is not clearly visible in the other longer and probably later narratives, such as Luke 24:13-35 and John 21. However, we have much to learn from these narratives about the nature of Christ's presence in the midst of his people. In this chapter we will focus on his presence with the two disciples on the road to Emmaus (Luke 24:13-35); in the next chapter we will concentrate on his presence by the lake (John 21).

The Emmaus story is an artistic gem. As Reginald Fuller has said so well, "To submit it to traditio-historical analysis seems irreverent, for any analysis will fail to capture its true spirit."[1] Having said this, Fuller does analyze it, and draws this conclusion: "The Emmaus story is thus a unique compendium of Easter traditions, the product of a considerable process of development. It may contain a basic nucleus of historical fact, if it can be identified with one of the appearances included among the appearances 'to all the apos-

1. Fuller, *The Formation of the Resurrection Narratives* (New York: Macmillan, 1971), p. 104.

tles' and especially if the name Clopas warrants some
connection with James."² Others agree that it is unique and
significantly Lukan,³ ranging from H. D. Betz, who calls it a
"cult legend" with a theological purpose,⁴ to those who see
it as a self-contained and originally independent story concerning a manifestation of the risen Lord.⁵

There is no way to know for certain whether an actual
appearance lies behind it or to what extent it is the product
of the pen of the author of Luke. However, it is so true to
the experience of the church today that it has the ring of
historical authenticity. To call it a "cult legend" serves no
purpose and is unnecessarily skeptical in my judgment. In
any event, the narrative is theologically consistent with the
other narratives, it is a fruitful paradigm for Christian self-
understanding, and it cannot be demonstrated to be late
historically. So let us proceed to listen to it.

THE SETTING

Two disciples, one named Cleopas, are with "the eleven and
. . . all the rest" (v. 9) in Jerusalem, where they hear the
testimony of the women who have visited the tomb. This
witness "amazes" the two. They say that "some of those who
were with us went to the tomb, and found it just as the
women had said; but him (Jesus as Lord) they did not see"
(v. 24). They may agree with the others that the women's
testimony "seemed . . . an idle tale" (v. 12). In any case, they
are "sad-faced" (skuthrōpoi) (v. 17) and apparently think the
crucifixion to be the last word, though they "had hoped that
he (Jesus) was the one to redeem Israel" (v. 21).

2. Fuller, *The Formation of the Resurrection Narratives*, p. 113.
3. Richard J. Dillon, *From Eye-witnesses to Ministers of the Word: Tradition and Composition in Luke 24* (Rome: Biblical Institute Press, 1978), p. 144.
4. Betz, "The Origin and Nature of Christian Faith According to the Emmaus Legend (Luke 24:13-32)," *Interpretation* 23 (1969): 33-34.
5. Arnold Ehrhardt, "The Disciples of Emmaus," *New Testament Studies* 10 (1963-64): 183.

Walking on the road from Jerusalem to Emmaus, they engage in warm conversation, maybe debate *(homileō)*, about "all these things that had happened" (v. 14); about "Jesus of Nazareth, who was a prophet mighty in deed and word before God and all the people" (v. 19); about his condemnation at the hands of the chief priests and rulers and his subsequent crucifixion (v. 20). Three days have passed, and even the witness of the empty tomb has not given them hope (vv. 21-25).

THE PRESENCE

On the road they meet Jesus, whom they do not recognize (vv. 15-16), and they share their news with him. To them the Present One is a stranger. The narrator tells us that "their eyes were kept (held) from recognizing him" (v. 16). Recognition or awareness of who is present awaits his identifying himself. It is not apparent that the Present One is Lord and Christ. This is consistent with the three narratives discussed in the last chapter. However, the response of the two to his presence is brought about not by a sign of the cross or a simple word but by something even more significant for our understanding.

Present as He Interpreted the Scriptures

Jesus the Lord responds to the sad-faced disciples rather strongly: "O foolish men, and slow of heart to believe all that the prophets have spoken!" (v. 25). It is clear that they have failed to understand that his suffering and death were necessary in order that he "enter into his glory" (v. 26). They have mistakenly believed that the "one to redeem Israel" (v. 21) could not be the one who "suffer(ed) these things" (v. 26). The Present One then reveals that Jesus of Nazareth, the "prophet mighty in deed and word" who suffered and was crucified, did so in order to redeem Israel and now is entering into glory. He makes the connection for them: "Beginning with Moses and all the prophets, he interpreted to them in all the scriptures the things concerning himself" (v. 27). This is also described as "opening (to us) the scriptures" (v. 32).

This is very central to our understanding of the presence of Jesus as Lord. The narrator (the author of Luke or of an earlier tradition, or the two disciples themselves through an oral tradition) has come to understand, first of all, the truth that the Scriptures (meaning the Old Testament) reveal who Jesus is. The Scriptures are about Jesus, the "prophet mighty in deed and word" who suffered and died to redeem Israel. The revelation, the insight, is that all Scripture points to Jesus, now glorified as Lord. Second, he, the Re-created One, is the interpreter of Scripture for the church. He is present to and with the church in and as the Interpretation of Scripture. Third, his life and ministry are understood retrospectively—that is, from the vantage point of the re-creation, from Emmaus looking back.

When Scripture is read and heard, even debated, Christ is present in the process as the norm of interpretation, even as the author of interpretation. In my judgment, this truth, which is central to our faith, could hardly have been the result of solitary contemplation or even vigorous debate in the early community of the church. It was so startling and new and revolutionary that it seems more reasonable to believe that the disciples came to this truth by way of an encounter with their Lord. But it should be noted that the two disciples did not recognize the stranger as Jesus until "he was known to them in the breaking of the bread" (v. 35; see the following section for explication). As the story is told, Scripture was understood to be about him only after the two encountered him in the breaking of the bread. Arnold Ehrhardt, writing in *New Testament Studies* about this passage, concludes, "I feel convinced that it was the instruction given by the risen Christ to his disciples about the witness of the Old Testament which was turned by John

v. 39 into the dominical command, 'search the scriptures
. . . and it is they that witness about me.'"6

H. D. Betz also writes of the presence of Jesus Christ in
the word as interpreted in the Emmaus story:

> Jesus is present wherever there are people who raise ques-
> tions about him, who contemplate and discuss his signifi-
> cance. Of course he is present even when these conversations
> reflect doubt, unbelief, and disappointment. Although the
> legend itself describes his presence as mysterious and super-
> natural, its intention is not to imply that it is simply myste-
> rious or supernatural. Rather the mythological concepts in-
> tend to show that the resurrected Jesus is present in his word
> and by his word as a partner in a conversation.7

Though I consider the concepts of "myth" and "legend"
misleading, and have little difficulty believing that the Emmaus story goes back to an historic encounter, I otherwise
agree with Betz's conclusion. Jesus as Lord is present in his
word and by his word and in the process of our interpretation of that word. This is an indispensable truth for understanding Scripture and preaching and Bible study. The
witness of the Emmaus disciples is "Did not our hearts burn
within us while he talked to us on the road, while he opened
to us the scriptures?" (24:32). That is the experience of
Christians since then, of countless thousands who have
known Christ present in Scripture in public worship, infor-
mal conversation, and private meditation.

Present in the Breaking of the Bread

As important as the "opening of scriptures" is for our understanding the appearance to the disciples on the Emmaus
road, the crux of the story is "how he was known to them in

6. Ehrhardt, "The Disciples of Emmaus," p. 189.
7. Betz, "The Origin and Nature of Christian Faith According to the
Emmaus Legend," p. 40.

the breaking of the bread" (v. 35). The disciples draw near to Emmaus, and the unrecognized stranger appears "to be going further" (v. 28). They urge him to stay with them; it is almost in the form of a prayer: "Stay with us, for it is toward evening and the day is now far spent" (v. 29). (The earliest of Christian prayers seems to be *"Maranatha,"* "O Lord, come!" A mealtime prayer attributed to Martin Luther picks up this language and theme: "Come, O Lord, and be our guest, and bless what thou hast given us.") Prayer or not, "he went in to stay with them" (v. 29). Then and only then do they recognize him: "When he was at table with them, he took the bread and blessed, and broke it, and gave it to them. And their eyes were opened and they recognized him; and he vanished out of their sight" (vv. 30-31). They think back to their conversation on the road, now understanding its powerful effect: "Did not our hearts burn within us while he talked to us on the road, while he opened to us the scriptures?" (v. 32). They get up from the table and set out for Jerusalem, where they find the eleven gathered together and tell them "what had happened on the road, and how he was known to them in the breaking of the bread" (v. 35).

The stranger is recognized; the eyes of the two are opened, and they know the Lord Jesus to be present as bread is: taken, blessed, broken, and given to them. Members of Christian communities that center on eucharistic worship then and now would recognize immediately the action, which has come to be known as the "fourfold shape" of the Eucharist—take, bless, break, and give. Many commentators (Oscar Cullmann, Joachim Jeremias, and others)[8] believe that the narrator is clearly identifying the context of this appearance as eucharistic with the words *en tē klasei tou artou,* "in the breaking of the bread" (v. 35). In

---

8. See Cullmann, *Early Christian Worship* (London: SCM Press, 1953), pp. 14-15; Jeremias, *The Eucharistic Words of Jesus* (New York: Macmillan, 1955), pp. 82-83; and Jacques DuPont, "The Meal at Emmaus," in *The Eucharist in the New Testament* (London: Geoffrey Chapman, 1965), pp. 117-18.

Acts 2:42 the worship life of the earliest church is described in similar words: "And they devoted themselves to the apostles' teaching and fellowship, to the breaking of bread *(tē klasei tou artou)* and the prayers." They broke bread "with glad and generous hearts" (Acts 2:46), perhaps translated as "exuberant joy."[9]

The commentators cited agree that the author of Luke-Acts used this language as a clear reference to the eucharistic worship of the earliest church, certainly to that of the church at the time of the writing of Luke-Acts and probably to that of an earlier church. In their view, the reference is not to an ordinary meal, not even to one taken in common. The action of Luke 24:30 is quite close to that which Paul describes in 1 Corinthians 11:23-26, written 25-35 years earlier. Paul says that he "received from the Lord what I also delivered to you (the Corinthian Christians), that the Lord Jesus on the night when he was betrayed took bread, and when he had given thanks, he broke it, and said, 'This is my body which is for you. Do this in remembrance of me.'" (Similar passages are Mark 14:22; Matthew 26:26; and Luke 22:19. Some of these passages use "blessed" *(eulogēsen)*, as does the Emmaus story, and others use "gave thanks" *(eucharistēsas)*, but the language and shape of the special meal at which Christ presides is quite evident in all of them. The meal at Emmaus at which the Lord is present is thus identified with the supper on the night before he died and with the eucharistic meal of the earliest Christians at worship. Oscar Cullmann interprets the connection:

> The first eucharistic feasts of the community look back to the Easter meals, in which the Messianic meal promised by Jesus at the Last Supper was already partly anticipated. Just how closely the thought of the resurrection in general was linked with the recollection of those Easter meals shared with the Christ of the appearances can be gauged from Acts 10:40, where in Peter's address we read: "This Christ God

9. Cullmann, *Early Christian Worship*, p. 15.

raised up the third day and gave him to be made manifest, not to all the people but unto witnesses that were chosen before of God, even to us who did eat and drink with Him after He rose from the dead."[10]

Cullmann is referring not only to the Emmaus story but to the recording of the other occasions on which the Christ appeared to the disciples during a meal[11]—namely, Luke 24:41-43 and John 21:12-13.

Jesus was known as Lord, present to the disciples after his death as they took bread, blessed or gave thanks over it, broke it, and distributed it. The Emmaus story links his eucharistic presence to an appearance soon after his death. Recognition, the opening of eyes to his identity, came in making the connection between the Lord who was present and the Jesus who presided in a similar way on the night before he died. Here Christ reveals himself not by showing his wounds as a sign of the cross but by repeating the action of the Last Supper, which he had asked his disciples to do in remembrance of him.

I realize that it is possible to understand the Emmaus narrative in alternative ways. Thus in composing the Emmaus story the author of Luke could have used, rather intentionally, the language of the eucharistic meal of the church (as discussed on pp. 64-65 herein). Still another view is the cautious approach of Reginald Fuller:

> There is no apparent reason why the eucharistic meal should not have provided the occasion for some at least of the resurrection appearances, more probably those which occurred to groups rather than those to single individuals. When the Christian community began to *narrate* appearances, it may have modeled its narrations on the meals which Jesus celebrated with his disciples during his earthly ministry (e.g., *he* pronounces the blessing). Next, it de-

10. Cullmann, *Early Christian Worship*, pp. 15-16.
11. Cullmann, *Early Christian Worship*, p. 15.

veloped these eucharistic appearances in the interest of
apologetic (the risen Lord is made to eat in front of the
disciples as a demonstration of the physical reality of his
risen manifestation).[12]

I believe that Oscar Cullmann makes the most sense of the
connection of the Last Supper, the appearance of the re-
created Lord among the disciples gathered together for a
meal, and the eucharistic worship-meal of the earliest
church: "This Last Supper of the historical Jesus is certainly
the original source of the community Feast, in so far as it
was in remembrance of that Last Supper that the disciples
came together after the resurrection to eat the meal at
which the risen Christ appeared to them."[13]

The Christian community of the author of Luke knew
Christ as present in the breaking of the bread, as we do now
and as the disciples at Emmaus did. Of these meals where
Christ's presence was known, Cullmann says,

> The emphasis laid on the presence of the risen Christ at
> these early meals is in keeping with the fact established
> above [in his discussion] that the first Christians chose the
> day of Christ's resurrection as the day for the service of
> worship, and conforms also with the whole central meaning
> of the prayer *Maranatha*. The term "Lord's Supper" (I Cor.
> 11:20) also points in this direction.[14]

What does it all mean? H. D. Betz offers this explanation
of the meaning of the Emmaus passage: "His miraculous
disappearance shows the way in which he will be present
from now on. The presence of the resurrected Lord Jesus is
hereby clearly defined: He is present in the act of the Christian interpretation of the Scriptures and in the act of the
Lord's Supper." Betz adds, "According to the Emmaus leg-

12. Fuller, *The Formation of the Resurrection Narratives*, p. 109.
13. Cullmann, *Early Christian Worship*, p. 18.
14. Cullmann, *Early Christian Worship*, pp. 16-17.

end, it is the presence of the crucified Jesus which makes Christian faith possible."[15]

Christ's presence to the earliest apostolic witnesses made faith possible for them. He was present, and they believed. So also for the community for whom the author of Luke is writing, and so also for us. The Emmaus story helps us to recognize and identify the Present One as the Lord Jesus Christ.

He was present to the two disciples in the breaking of the bread and in the interpretation of Scripture, and their "hearts burned within them." Later Christians gathered to share his presence as bread was broken, and shared it "with glad and generous hearts" or "exuberant joy." I use the word "share" advisedly. Hans-Georg Gadamer in *Truth and Method* says of presence at a feast or festival, "To be present does not mean simply to be in the presence of something else that is there at the same time. To be present means to share."[16] The disciples at Emmaus, like those on the mountaintop and those gathered together in the locked room, shared in his presence. And they went out into the world to share his presence with others through their teaching and preaching and acts of healing and by bringing others into the fellowship of his presence, particularly as he was known to be present in the breaking of the bread.

In *Jesus the Christ* Walter Kasper notes, "He appears to them while going away. . . . He is not to be conjured up in his appearances; he manifests himself in his departure, he comes as one who is going away."[17] So also his church knows him as it makes him known, knows his presence as it goes forth to share his presence with the world.

15. Betz, "The Origin and Nature of Christian Faith According to the Emmaus Legend," pp. 37-39.

16. Gadamer, *Truth and Method* (New York: Seabury Press, 1975), pp. 110-11.

17. Kasper, *Jesus the Christ* (New York: Paulist Press, 1976), p. 139.

CHAPTER 6

The Appearance by the Lake: Feed My Sheep

JOHN 21

In the appearance by the lake in the twenty-first chapter of John we have neither a succinct pericope such as those described earlier, with the common pattern so clearly evident, nor do we have a story with the art and internal unity of the Emmaus narrative. We have instead a chapter variously called a supplement, an appendix, or an epilogue, possibly written by an editor rather than by the evangelist himself.[1] Raymond E. Brown believes, as do most commentators, that the Gospel of John never circulated without the twenty-first chapter, but that the chapter is "an addition to the Gospel, consisting of a once independent narrative of Jesus' appearance to his disciples."[2] Reginald Fuller believes that it should be attributed to the school of the evangelist, not to the author of chapters 1-20.[3] There is much disagreement about the chapter's source(s). Much is made of the affinities between the narrative of the miraculous catch of fish in Luke 5:1-11 and the first part of chapter 21. Both Brown and Fuller, along with Joseph Fitzmyer, conclude that the Lukan narrative is originally a postresurrection story that Luke moved back into the narrative of Christ's earthly ministry.[4]

1. Raymond E. Brown, *The Gospel According to John XIII-XXI*, Anchor Bible, vol. 29A (Garden City, N.Y.: Doubleday, 1970), pp. 1078-80.
2. Brown, *The Gospel According to John XIII-XXI*, pp. 1077-78.
3. Fuller, *The Formation of the Resurrection Narratives* (New York: Macmillan, 1971), pp. 146-47.
4. See Brown, *The Gospel According to John XIII-XXI*, pp. 1090-92; and Fitzmyer, *The Gospel According to Luke I-IX*, Anchor Bible, vol. 28 (Garden City, N.Y.: Doubleday, 1981), pp. 560-61. Fuller revised his earlier opinion (p. 151) in the 1979 preface (p. viii) of *The Formation of the Resurrection Narratives* to agree with Brown.

John 21 may go back to an early tradition about the appearance to Peter that is not narrated elsewhere but only referred to in 1 Corinthians 15:5 and Luke 24:34. Despite the difficulties over the authorship of the chapter and its contradiction of chapter 20, Reginald Fuller says, "Of all the stories that have been examined so far, this story, late though it is, seems to be in closest touch with the primitive tradition. Its Galilean location, the meal motif (not a demonstration) and the foundation of the church under the supervision of Peter—all are features going back to Mark 16:7 and behind it to 1 Corinthians 15:5."[5] It may be a late creation of a redactor who knew of several traditions, including the one behind Luke 5:1-11 and possibly the Emmaus tradition.[6] I don't think it is possible or necessary to decide. What is important is that the Gospel of John as we now have it includes a narrative, purportedly of an appearance of the Lord by the lake, that is distinctive and that gives us important insights into the meaning of the recreation. At the very least it is the inspired perception of the late-first-century church of the meaning of the presence of Jesus as Christ among them; it could be based on a very early tradition of the "lost" appearance to Peter.

Let us look at the chapter. The narrator describes the appearance as a "revelation": "After this Jesus revealed himself again to the disciples by the Sea of Tiberias" (v. 1; see v. 14). The verb *phaneroō* is used elsewhere in John and means, according to Raymond Brown, "a concrete revelation of the heavenly upon earth."[7] Admittedly, this does not tell us much about the nature of the appearance, but the details of the passage will.

Simon Peter, now back in Galilee, announces, "I am going fishing" (v. 3), and six disciples (four named and two unnamed) join him (vv. 2-3). The chapter immediately fol-

5. Fuller, *The Formation of the Resurrection Narratives*, p. 153.
6. Ulrich Wilckens, *Resurrection: Biblical Testimony to the Resurrection—An Historical Examination and Explication*, trans. A. M. Stewart (Atlanta: John Knox Press, 1978), pp. 59-62.
7. Brown, *The Gospel According to John XIII-XXI*, p. 1067.

lows the narration of appearances of Jesus as Lord and the sending forth of the disciples into the world in the name of Christ Risen and in the power of the spirit. Thus it is odd, to say the least, that the mission has been dropped for a return to fishing. This is one of the more obvious reasons for the dispute over the historical roots of the narrative and over its placement as a post-Easter event. The most appealing solution is that the narrative intends to be about the first appearance to Peter and was not known to the evangelist, who, had he known of it, might have placed it right after the narrative of the empty tomb. In this case, the speculation runs, the discouraged disciples returned from Jerusalem, not having seen Christ, and went back to their former vocation, only to encounter their Lord by the lake where they had first known him.[8] But this is only speculation. It is not possible to give a single or even a very good interpretation of the return to fishing.

They catch nothing (v. 3). Jesus stands on the beach, "yet the disciples did not know that it was Jesus" (v. 4). He calls to them, "Children (perhaps 'Friends' [NEB] or 'Lads,' according to Raymond Brown),[9] have you any fish?" (v. 5). They answer "no," and he instructs them, "Cast the net on the right side of the boat, and you will find some" (v. 6). They do so, and the catch is so large that they can't haul it in (v. 6). This event—the catch, the voice, the command, perhaps—causes the Beloved Disciple to recognize Jesus, and he says to Peter, "It is the Lord!" (v. 7).

He is present, and he is recognized—not by a word, or through a sign of the cross (the wounds), or by interpretation of Scripture, or in the breaking of the bread (though that may be involved later in the narrative). He is recognized as the disciples catch a huge quantity of fish in response to his command. Nowhere else is recognition of the Present One brought about by such an unusual occurrence. It could be that it triggered the memory of their calling to be

8. Brown, *The Gospel According to John XIII-XXI*, p. 1092; and Fuller, *The Formation of the Resurrection Narratives*, pp. 148-49.
9. Brown, *The Gospel According to John XIII-XXI*, p. 1070.

"fishers of men," though this language does not occur in the Johannine tradition. Or the recognition might be attributed to the special quality of the faith of the Beloved Disciple, who believes, according to John 20:8, on the basis of the empty tomb alone.

Peter responds, impetuously as usual, and leaps into the water from the boat after putting on his outer garment (v. 7). The other disciples bring in the boat towing the net full of fish (v. 8). When they reach land, they see a charcoal fire, over which there is a fish and some bread (v. 9). Jesus tells them to "bring some of the fish that you have just caught" (v. 10), and Peter hauls the net in, "full of large fish, a hundred and fifty-three of them" (v. 11). There is endless speculation about this number. Does it represent one of every kind of fish then known to the ancient world, or some perfect number? After examining many proposed explanations, Raymond Brown concludes that this number "may be meant to symbolize the breadth or even the universality of the Christian mission."[10] Something is going on. In obedience to the command of the Lord, the disciples have landed a huge catch of fish, perhaps meant to be a perfect or a full catch. There is no specific command or call to mission as there is in the other appearance stories, only the mystery of a large catch.

But there is more. Jesus invites them to breakfast, and he "took the bread and gave it to them and so with the fish" (v. 13). Many believe, with Raymond Brown and Oscar Cullmann, that this is eucharistic language.[11] The language of Emmaus is, like that of the upper-room meal, about *bread* and *wine;* this is about *fish,* as are the feeding of the multitudes and the appearance in Luke 24:43. There is no "blessing" or "giving thanks," so the eucharistic connection is not obvious. At breakfast, we are told, "Now none of the disciples dared ask him, 'Who are you?' They knew it was the Lord" (v. 12). We have here the barest hint that recogni-

10. Brown, *The Gospel According to John XIII-XXI,* p. 1075.
11. Brown, *The Gospel According to John XIII-XXI,* pp. 1098-1100; and Cullmann, *Early Christian Worship* (London: SCM Press, 1953), pp. 15-17.

tion was not without some hesitation. Yet, they "knew." Why? Was it the testimony of the Beloved Disciple, or Peter's impetuous response, or the huge catch in response to his command after they had failed to catch anything, or the meal that was reminiscent of other meals with him? We don't know for certain. The reason for the recognition is not clear. The passage makes sense only when we read it in the light of other narratives of the appearance or of the miraculous catch in Luke 5:1-11, which includes these words to Peter: "Do not be afraid; henceforth you will be catching men" (v. 10).

It is only in the second part of the chapter that the passage adds anything significant to our understanding of the re-creation. The account of Peter's rehabilitation or reconciliation (vv. 15-19) supplements our understanding of the command found in the other passages. Here it is not "going and telling" or "teaching and witnessing." Here it is nurturing and loving. In John 20, as in Luke 24, the disciple is told to be an agent of God's forgiveness, through forgiveness bringing others into the community of the forgiven, the church. Here forgiveness is linked with love.

Jesus asks Peter, "Simon, son of John, do you love me more than these?" (v. 15). This probably means "Do you love me more than these other disciples do?" though some have conjectured that "these" refers to boats and returning to fishing.[12] Peter replies, "Yes, Lord; you know that I love you" (v. 15). Jesus says, "Feed my lambs" (v. 15). Three times Jesus asks the question; we are told that "Peter was grieved" (v. 17) because he was asked three times. Each time Jesus issues the same command—to feed his lambs or sheep. Two different words are used and translated as "love"—*agapas* and *philō*. Though frequently one is seen as a "higher" love and the other as a more conventional, "brotherly" love, Raymond Brown and others conclude that here the words are interchangeable.[13]

12. Brown, *The Gospel According to John XIII-XXI*, p. 1103-4.
13. Brown, *The Gospel According to John XIII-XXI*, p. 1103.

Simon Peter, who three times denied Jesus in the courtyard outside the place where Jesus was tried, is here three times forgiven and restored to relationship with the Lord. Only in John is the bond uniting the disciples to their Lord a bond of love. "Love one another even as I have loved you" (13:34). Here in John 21, obedience is love. Peter's love of the Lord who is present is to lead him to pastoral oversight. He is to "feed" and "tend" the sheep of Christ, "my" sheep. The Good Shepherd has now commissioned Peter as shepherd, perhaps chief shepherd. He is commanded to feed, tend, protect, and nurture the flock of Christ out of love for the Lord and in response to his love. Peter's apostasy required that his love be declared. (Note that Peter didn't insist on his own rectitude. He said that the Lord "knew" of his love before asking.)

The church has a mission not only to teach and baptize and forgive, but to tend and feed and nurture out of love and in love. Its mandate is both missionary and pastoral. This is clearly comprehended within the meaning of the re-creation.

After calling Peter to be a pastor, Jesus says to him, "Truly, truly, I say to you, when you were young, you girded yourself and walked where you would; but when you are old, you will stretch out your hands, and another will gird you and carry you where you do not wish to go" (v. 18). The narrator makes this parenthetical comment: "This he said to show by what death he was to glorify God" (v. 19). Like the old man who can no longer gird himself, Peter will be taken where he does not wish to go. Pastoring out of the love of the Lord will lead to martyrdom and death. Obviously, the kind of pastoring implied must go beyond the therapeutic because the role of consoler-counselor per se seldom leads to a martyr's death. It is only when public structures (the powers of this world) are confronted that martyrdom is involved. After this aside, Peter is called: "Follow me," Jesus says (v. 19).

Obedience to the command of the Lord is to respond out of love and to follow him, to love as he loves and to care for his sheep as he cares for them. Loving and caring may not result in being universally loved in return. That was not Jesus' reward, and it is not to be Peter's. Is it to be ours? We say, "The whole world loves a lover." Not necessarily. This is no wishy-washy love. Loving discipleship may end in death. Obviously the editor of the Gospel of John sees the twenty-first chapter in the context of that which goes before. He understands, as we should, that we love and tend and feed in the power of the love and abiding spirit of him who goes with us. We are called to "Follow him," not go forth in his absence. Though the ultimate destination may be going where we don't want to go, we go with him nonetheless. So the command "Follow me" is both a call and a promise.

CHAPTER 7

Do Not Hold Me . . . But Go to My Brethren: The Appearance to Mary Magdalene and the Women

According to Matthew and John, the first appearance of the Christ to any followers is to women among his disciples (Matt. 28:9-10; John 20:11-18). The appearance to the women in Matthew is but two verses in length; the appearance to Mary Magdalene in John is a more elaborate story. Reginald Fuller believes that the Matthew pericope is based on an earlier tradition available to Matthew but later than the traditions behind the empty-tomb narrative in Mark or the list of appearances in Paul.[1] His principal arguments for relative lateness are the "materialization" of the appearance and Paul's failure to mention the appearance to the women. (The latter could be for reasons similar to those that explain the failure of the male disciples to believe the report of the women about the empty tomb—namely, that the testimony of women was not to be accepted.) On the other hand, as we will see in the discussion of the appearance to Mary in John's Gospel, some commentators (such as C. H. Dodd and Raymond E. Brown) believe that these accounts may be quite early.

Let us look first at the account in Matthew: "And behold, Jesus met them and said, 'Hail!' And they came up and took hold of his feet and worshiped him. Then Jesus said to

---

1. Fuller, *The Formation of the Resurrection Narratives* (New York: Macmillan, 1971), pp. 77-79.

them, 'Do not be afraid; go and tell my brethren to go to Galilee, and there they will see me'" (28:9-10).

We are in the same narrative world as Matthew 28:16-20, with simple, stark narration. There is no description—only "Jesus met them and said, 'Hail!'" The word of greeting *(chairete)* is the everyday street greeting of the Hellenistic world,[2] the equivalent of "Peace be with you" in the Jewish community. The women respond to his word by "worshiping" him (literally "falling on their faces") and by taking hold of his feet. He says, "Do not be afraid." Here, as in the other brief narratives of the appearances, the recognition includes both worship and fear. There is, however, no failure to recognize the One present as Jesus. (As we have seen, nonrecognition has been typical of the appearance narratives, and figures in John's account of Mary Magdalene's meeting with Christ.) There is also no element of doubt. I can find no plausible explanation for these differences. We are not told what the women saw, only that they heard a simple word of greeting and that they were told not to fear. The emphasis is clearly on the word. They hear him, and they know him.

The command is simple: "Go and tell my brethren to go to Galilee, and there they will see me" (v. 10). The command is the essence of the more detailed commands we have been examining: "Go and tell." However, as in the command to the women at the tomb (see pp. 22-23 herein), the women are sent only to the disciples. Note that the disciples are Christ's "brethren" *(adelphois)*. In Matthew, "brethren" is clearly "brothers," as the appearance in Galilee on the mountain is to "the eleven," who, as we know, are all male. In John 20:11-18, where Mary is also told to "go to my brethren" (John 20:17), the appearance that follows is in the midst of "the disciples" (20:19). This is possibly ambiguous and might include the women. In Luke there is

2. C. H. Dodd, "The Appearances of the Risen Christ: An Essay in Form-Criticism of the Gospels," in *More New Testament Studies* (Grand Rapids: Eerdmans, 1968), p. 105.

no separate appearance to the women, and no use of "brethren," but the women at the tomb tell what they have seen to "the apostles" (24:10) and apparently to other disciples as well, since the two on the road to Emmaus refer to the report by "some women of our company" (24:22). Jesus then appears to "the eleven gathered together and those who were with them" (24:33). The language describing the appearances to the assembled group in Luke and John allows an interpretation that includes the presence of the women; therefore, we are not doing violence to the narrative by interpreting "brethren"—at least in John—as inclusive of women as well as men. Furthermore, as I have pointed out (see p. 45 and p. 51 herein), Christ's intimate followers are no longer only disciples but "brothers" and "friends."

Christ is present; he is recognized by his word. The women respond in worship and fear. They hear and obey his command to "Go and tell." There is no promise.

In John 20:11-18 we are in a very different narrative world, but one with some parallels to the brief Matthew passage—the attempt to hold on to Jesus and the use of "brethren" in the command. To C. H. Dodd, it "feels" firsthand:

> This story never came out of any common stock of tradition; it has an arresting individuality. We seem to be shut up to two alternatives. Either we have here a free, imaginative composition based upon the bare tradition of an appearance to Mary Magdalen, akin to that represented by Matthew xxviii.9-10, or else the story came through some highly individual channel directly from the source, and the narrator stood near enough to catch the *nuances* of the original experience. It would be hazardous to dogmatize. The power to render psychological traits imaginatively, with convincing insight, cannot be denied to a writer to whom we owe the masterly character-parts of Pontius Pilate and the Woman of Samaria. Yet I confess that I cannot for long rid myself of the feeling (it can be no more than a feeling) that this *pericopé* has something indefinably first-hand about it. It

stands in any case alone. There is nothing quite like it in the gospels. Is there anything quite like it in all ancient literature?[3]

Raymond Brown concludes, "Therefore, despite the lateness of the witnesses, we are inclined to believe that the tradition of the appearance to Magdalene may be ancient."[4] In all the Gospels Mary Magdalene is certainly given primacy in the lists of the women followers of Jesus, even over the mother of the Lord. Brown thinks that "this may well be because she was the first one to see the risen Jesus."[5] This would obviously fly in the face of the primacy of the appearance to Peter and would be an embarrassment in view of the apparent fact that the disciples did not seem to believe the word of the women, presumably including Mary Magdalene. Reginald Fuller believes that John 20:11-18 is a "late story,"[6] but as we have seen, he suggests that the empty-tomb narrative may be "derived from a report given by Mary Magdalene to the disciples."[7]

I have gone on at some length, but not to "prove" the historicity of the accounts of the appearances to the women, though I have no difficulty with that view. Rather, my intention is to suggest that we should take seriously the possibility of the primacy of the appearance of the re-created Lord to Mary Magdalene and the other women as is so obviously the case with the discovery of the empty tomb. The early church may not have given primacy of leadership to women, but the Lord may have appeared to them first and thereby given evangelical primacy to them. They were most likely the first to hear and obey the command to "go and tell" the good news.

A few details of the appearance to Mary Magdalene are

3. Dodd, "The Appearances of the Risen Christ," p. 115.

4. Brown, *The Gospel According to John XIII-XXI*, Anchor Bible, vol. 29A (Garden City, N.Y.: Doubleday, 1970), p. 1003.

5. Brown, *The Gospel According to John XIII-XXI*, p. 1003.

6. Fuller, *The Formation of the Resurrection Narratives*, p. 137.

7. See pp. 25-26 herein.

worth exploring. She is weeping outside the empty tomb. The Beloved Disciple may have seen the tomb empty and gone away "believing." Mary, however, is weeping "because they have taken away my Lord, and I do not know where they have laid him" (John 20:13). Neither the empty tomb nor a vision of angels has caused Mary Magdalene to believe that Jesus is Lord. She looks up from her weeping and sees a man whom she supposes "to be the gardener" (v. 15). She asks him to tell her "where you have laid him." He addresses her by name: "Mary." Only then does she recognize him and respond "Rabboni" (v. 16), which John translates for us as "teacher." Note that the figure she sees is described as a "gardener," not a "spirit" or a "phantom"—nor, however, a person recognizable as Jesus. Jesus as Lord is recognized not by seeing but in hearing the word—here, in the calling of Mary's name. We are reminded of the earlier discourse in John 10 about the shepherd who "calls his own sheep by name and leads them out. . . . The sheep follow him, for they know his voice" (vv. 3-4). He is the "good shepherd" who "lays down his life for the sheep" (v. 11); he knows his own, and they know him (v. 14).

Hearing her name, Mary recognizes Jesus and, as in the account in Matthew 28:9-10, responds by attempting to hold him. The words *mē mou haptou* may be read as "Stop clinging to me"[8] or "Don't cling to me." In either case we have a rather physical presence implied, but of a person whose identity is not perceived by sight.

Jesus tells Mary, "Go to my brethren and say to them, I am ascending to my Father and your Father, to my God and your God" (v. 17). We know from what follows in John that Jesus as Lord is to be known in the midst of the disciples and that no ascension is narrated in John's Gospel. What is going on here? Raymond Brown believes that we are being told that Jesus is "all ready in the process of ascending, but has not yet reached his ultimate destination," which is to be with the Father. According to Brown, "In telling her [Mary]

8. Fuller, *The Formation of the Resurrection Narratives*, p. 138; and Brown, *The Gospel According to John XIII-XXI*, p. 992.

not to hold on to him, Jesus indicates that his permanent presence is not by way of appearance, but by way of the gift of the Spirit that can come only after he has ascended to the Father." Following a suggestion of Bultmann, Brown says further, "'I have not yet ascended' is really applicable to Magdalene's desire—she cannot yet have Jesus' enduring presence. Instead of trying to hold on to Jesus . . . she is commanded to go and prepare his disciples for that coming of Jesus when the Spirit will be given."[9]

This is similar to my conclusion (see p. 43 and pp. 46-47 herein) regarding the relation between the presence and the command in the brief appearance narratives, those that narrate traditions of the seminal encounter between the Lord and the assembled disciples. Disciples, then and now, cannot remain in Christ's presence perpetually. We cannot hold him, or we will lose him. Mary had to let him go; so did the eleven, and so do we. We are called to go out from his presence to tell the brethren and in the name of the brethren to tell the world that Jesus is Lord. They and we are to tell the world that he is not held captive in the church either in the sacraments or in Scripture. He is loose in the world, where we are commanded to follow. Mary, obedient to his commands, goes and tells the disciples, "I have seen the Lord" (v. 18). We too can go out from his presence in the midst of the brethren gathered in his name and witness to the truth that we have encountered the Lord. We will not use the word "seen," as Mary did, but we who have not seen are nonetheless "blessed" (v. 29). We believe that he has been present in our midst, and we can attest to that truth.

Mary Magdalene and the women are likely the first witnesses to the presence of Jesus as Lord, and we are grateful for their witness.[10] It was the central apostolic role, and it remains so for the Christian today.

9. Brown, *The Gospel According to John XIII-XXI*, pp. 994, 1012.

10. For an interesting discussion of the primacy of Mary Magdalene as a witness to the resurrection, see Elisabeth Schüssler Fiorenza, *In Memory of Her: A Feminist Theological Reconstruction of Christian Origins* (New York: Crossroad, 1984).

CHAPTER 8

The Presence of Jesus as Lord—
Then and Now

I have looked at the Easter texts, the central New Testament texts for understanding the appearance of Jesus as Lord among his followers in the period beginning immediately after his death and probably terminating with his appearance to Paul several years later. I have set forth a case for understanding three brief narratives of the appearance to the assembled disciples that I believe provide a window into the seminal encounter, the appearance "to the twelve" or perhaps the appearance "to all the apostles." An analysis of these three concise passages has provided us with a structure for understanding the nature of the encounter with the Re-created One and has been used to help us understand the other narratives of his appearance. These (the appearance to the disciples on the Emmaus road, to the disciples by the lake, and to the women) have added to our understanding of the nature of his presence among his followers in that distinct and unique period following his death. I have suggested that a pattern is discernable in these appearance narratives that is quite obvious in the three central passages. Further, I have proposed that this pattern is a paradigm for our understanding of the nature of his presence among us and for our self-understanding of the nature of our faithful response to his presence.

In this chapter I will briefly summarize the points of the previous chapters and draw a few conclusions from them. Then I will address the question, How does our experience of Christ's presence compare with and differ from that of the original witnesses? In the following chapter I will look at the paradigm more closely.

THE PRESENCE AMONG THE ORIGINAL WITNESSES

Of the original witnesses to the presence, Saint Paul is the only eyewitness to write of his encounter with the Lord. The other encounters, as I have discussed at length, moved from oral traditions to written narratives over an extended period of time. Despite the differences in language and setting, there is considerable agreement among them.

First, in all the narratives *someone* is present among the disciples, to them and with them.

Second, only personal language is appropriate to describe the Present One. Perhaps he is a gardener or a stranger, but he is always a person.

Third, this person present is external to the witness, external to the consciousness of the witness. Paul in his use of the word "appear" *(ōpthē)* is speaking of the presence of someone apart from himself (see pp. 12-14 herein). The narratives of the appearances are also quite clear on this point: "Jesus came and stood among them." The original witnesses are not talking of an event that is purely internal and subjective. They are speaking of meeting someone external to themselves.

Fourth, the perception of the identity of the One who is present is not immediate nor obvious nor inevitable. There is doubt about who is present in many of the narratives, and false perceptions in some (Christ is thought to be a gardener or a stranger). The witnesses, including Paul in the narratives in Acts, do not immediately identify the Present One as Jesus. There is not only doubt but fear and wonder. They did not expect Jesus and are bewildered by his presence. They are not immediately able to comprehend that it is Jesus who is present.

Fifth, the Present One, though he has a personal identity, is nonetheless not in human form. He appears and disappears at will; he may come through closed doors; he may come as bright light. He is thought to be a spirit *(pneuma)*.

He is most probably in a "glorified body" rather than "flesh and blood."

Sixth, the Present One is finally perceived by the witnesses to be none other than Jesus who was crucified. Paul, who has never seen Jesus before, is convinced he has seen Jesus. In the Gospel appearance narratives, too, the Present One is identified as Jesus after various signs of identity: his words ("Peace be with you"), the signs of the cross (his wounds), his personal address ("Mary"). The witnesses proclaim "Jesus is risen," "Jesus is the Christ," and "Jesus is Lord." They come to know and believe—no matter how it staggers the imagination and shatters expectations—that the Present One is Jesus, who taught and traveled with them, who was crucified, dead, and buried. No one before has been re-created after death. But it is nonetheless Jesus who is present.

Seventh, this Jesus who is present is *Lord*. This conclusion is as radical as the knowledge that it is Jesus who is present. When Paul and the evangelists use "Lord" in reference to Jesus, they are using language usually reserved for God. When Paul refers to him as "Lord" and the early witnesses say "We have seen the Lord" (John 20:25), they are not simply using a proper name or a conventional appellation. They are speaking the unspeakable, perhaps in an unsophisticated way. They are identifying Jesus and God in some way. John goes all the way when he says, "My Lord and my God!" (20:28). Paul is very clear that "Lord" is not just an appellation when he quotes the creedal declaration "Jesus is Lord": "No one can say 'Jesus is Lord' except by the Holy Spirit" (1 Cor. 12:3).[1] A person is present; that person is Jesus, and that person is the Lord. Jesus is Lord and has come among them.

Eighth, the disciples respond to the Present One, to Jesus as Lord, in the only manner appropriate—they fall down

---

1. Hans Conzelmann, *First Corinthians: A Critical and Historical Commentary on the Bible*, trans. James W. Leitch, ed. George W. MacRae (Philadelphia: Fortress Press, 1975), pp. 23, 206n.22.

and worship him. They are filled with fear, holy fear, which is appropriate in the presence of the Lord. They are bewildered but joyful. The women cling to his feet, which is probably also a form of worship. The response to his presence is the awe and fear and worship one might expect in the presence of God.

The Holy One is present; he deserves to be addressed as "Lord," and the Lord is identified with Jesus who was crucified. He is apart from them. They worship him who is external to them. His presence causes them to throw themselves down on their faces. We may wish to rationalize this, but it is their witness and testimony nonetheless.

They knew that "no one has ever seen God." Moses had taught them that you cannot see God and live. Yet they spoke the unspeakable. They had "seen the Lord." They knew that no one had returned from death, yet they proclaimed that "Jesus is risen." We do not know whether a "glorious body" caused them to know the Lord was present, or whether the realization that Jesus was present and therefore created anew caused them to know that "Jesus was Lord." The overwhelming encounter led them to make the necessary connections, and they testified using the only language at hand, the language of resurrection. They said, "The Lord has risen indeed, and has appeared to Simon" (Luke 24:34), and "This Jesus God raised up, and of that we all are witnesses" (Acts 2:32).

I view resurrection language as metaphorical (see pp. 7-8 herein), not mythological (see p. 6 herein). Paul and the evangelists were speaking of a new creative act of God that brought a glorified Jesus into their midst. God, who can bring all that is into being, can certainly establish a new order of creation. By his power Jesus can be the first person to bridge the present order and the new order, to be, in Paul's words, "the second Adam." This should not strain Christian credulity. Nor does the testimony of the first witnesses violate contemporary science (see pp. 6-7 herein). A single event such as the re-creation can neither be predicted

nor ruled out by science. Science is mute on the subject but
not necessarily antagonistic to it, as earlier positivists have
asserted.

Presence as Command or Commission

The first witnesses were not only aware of the presence of
Jesus as Lord. They responded not only in reverence and
worship. They knew that they were sent forth; they understood themselves to be commissioned. (Here again the language of the passages varies, but this is not the central point,
as many critics agree.)

First, they knew themselves to be commissioned, called,
commanded to go forth in Jesus' name. They were "witnesses," "apostles," and "disciples." By whatever name, they
represented him and testified about him in the world.

Second, their going forth proceeded from his authority.
They did as he commanded; as he was sent, so they were
sent. It was not on their own initiative that they went out.

Third, there was specific content to their commission.
(Here there is more variety among the traditions, but they
do not contradict each other.) They were to make disciples
and teach what he had commanded (Matthew); they were to
be agents of forgiveness (John and Luke) and extensions of
his love (John 21). They were to bring others within the
circle of his teaching and love by baptism (explicit in Matthew and possibly implied in Luke and John).

Fourth, the mission was universal. They were commissioned to go to all nations (the commission is explicit in
Matthew and Luke and implied in John). Paul's mission to
the Gentiles also proceeded from his commissioning.

They knew Jesus as Lord and were commissioned in one
and the same act. His presence and command were part of a
single encounter. They saw him and heard him. They worshiped him and obeyed him. (In storytelling one must relate
events sequentially, but in reality these elements cannot be
ordered as neatly.) They knew he was sent from the Father
and that they were sent in his name. They knew that they

were forgiven and that they were agents of his forgiveness.
They knew that they were learners (disciples) and therefore
teachers. Their going forth preaching, teaching, forgiving,
and baptizing in his name was testimony to the reality of
their commissioning. Their obedience made effective his
command.

Presence as Promise

The first witnesses saw and worshiped, heard and obeyed,
accepted their commission and went forth. They did this
not only in response to his presence but also trusting in his
promise. Again there is much agreement among the traditions. Matthew uses the language of God's promise to
Moses: "I am with you always." According to John and
Luke, the promise is of the presence of the Spirit, clothing
them with power from on high. Three summary points are
in order.

First, the promise is Christ's promise, not a reiteration of
God's promise as a prophet might make. The promise proceeds from Jesus who is Lord: "I am with you always" (Matt.
28:20); "I send the promise of my Father upon you" (Luke
24:49); "He breathed on them, and said to them, 'Receive
the Holy Spirit'" (John 20:22). Jesus is Lord, and his promise is to be trusted.

Second, his presence is promised. He will be with them.
His breath infuses them with the Holy Spirit. He is revealed
in Holy Scripture and known in the breaking of bread. The
appearance narratives point to a Jesus-centered religion.
There is no getting around it. The re-creation is God's act,
but the command and the promise come from Jesus as
Lord, and the Presence that is promised is his. This is certainly qualified by much else in the New Testament (Jesus
proclaims the Kingdom of God, not himself, and so forth).
However, taken alone, these narratives are Jesus-centered.

Third, the presence that is promised is not limited to the
original witnesses. It extends to all nations and to the close
of the age. Where two or three are gathered together in his

name, he will be in their midst. The promise spans the ages
and is meant for us.

Again, the witnesses' knowing Jesus as Lord and knowing themselves to be sent forth in his name were part of one
single encounter and response. So also, trusting in the
promise of his continual presence cannot be separated
from the other two elements. They were emboldened to
obey his command as they trusted in his continued presence. He was with them and would go with them in spirit.
He commissioned them and empowered them to carry out
his command. They worshiped the Present One, Jesus as
Lord, and went forth in obedience to him, trusting his
promise.

Response as Faithfulness

The first witnesses testified to the presence among them, a
presence outside of themselves, which was seen as Jesus and
heard as Lord. They responded in adoration, obedience,
and trust. Their response gave credence to their testimony.
Their faithfulness is what the world saw; their explanation
of their behavior is what the world heard. They said that
they did what they did in obedience to the Lord's command.
They said that he had been present in his glory and that he
was still present in his spirit. They showed forth obedience
and trust. They worshiped not only the God of their fathers
but the God made known to them in their encounter with
the Lord Jesus. Their fidelity—unto death, in some cases—
and their testimony as contained in our Scripture is what
empirical evidence we have. It is fully in history and open to
inspection. As with anyone's explanation of his or her behavior, there is no certainty. But unless the behavior is in-
congruent with his or her testimony or contradicted by
other evidence, we must give it great weight, though it is still
only probable, not certain. So also with the testimony of the
first witnesses to the presence of Jesus as Lord. They explained their fidelity by witnessing to his presence and testifying to his promise. They said they acted out of obedience.

Other explanations for their conduct are possible, but we have relied on their testimony because it is congruent with our own experience of the Lord's presence.

The stance of adoration, obedience, and trust is what I believe faith is. The first Christians responded faithfully to Jesus as Lord. It was not an act of intellectual assent to the proposition "Jesus is Lord." It was a personal act of worshipful commitment and trust; it was a going forth motivated by adoration born out of the presence of the Lord Jesus. In traditional language, his grace preceded their faith. Presence begat adoration, command gave rise to obedience, and promise elicited trust. The graceful presence of Jesus as Lord called forth faithfulness, specifically seen as worship, obedience, and trust.

THE PRESENCE AMONG US

The faithfulness of the witnesses was born of their special encounter with Jesus as Lord. All of them were privileged to know him present in a manner and mode (what Paul calls "the glorified body") that was unique. Furthermore, these appearances were limited to a special period of time. Paul and the other witnesses are testifying not to a universal experience but to a special experience limited to a few people and a short length of time. This and the fact that most witnesses knew Jesus before the cross makes their experience of the presence of Jesus as Lord distinct and different from ours. We know him as present; if we did not, we would have little reason to take their witness seriously. But without their experience and testimony, we would have no way of interpreting our experience. We don't have faith in their faith, but our fidelity to Jesus as Lord is certainly dependent on their unique witness.

We now turn to the hard question: How does our experience of his presence differ from that of the original witnesses? Two important distinctions mentioned above should be underlined.

First, we have not known Jesus before the cross. We have only the portraits painted by the evangelists, who see him not as modern biographers do but in the light of the new creation. In order to identify him, we are dependent on the New Testament testimony.

Second, he does not appear to us in a "glorified body" as he did to the original witnesses. They can say with Paul that they "saw the Lord Jesus." We may say that we know him but not that we "saw" him. I do not wish to reduce their seeing to "insight" in order to make our seeing equal to theirs.

In John's Gospel a benediction is bestowed on those who come after the original witnesses: "Blessed are those who have not seen and yet believe" (20:29). We have not "seen" in the sense that they have. For them seeing can lead to believing. However, seeing does not equal believing, as in the modern empirical sense of the expression "Seeing is believing." We have noted that in the appearance stories, seeing led to ambiguous results. The witnesses identified Jesus as Lord not only by sight but by hearing as well. Sight alone often led to mistaken identity, and there was doubt even after seeing and hearing.

But for us, seeing is not involved, at least not in the basic sense of the word. Yet we are blessed! We are not second-class followers. Nevertheless, we may know him as present among us, but not by sight. Thus the eyes of the first witnesses are essential for us. They made an identification we cannot make, the identification of *Jesus* as Lord. We have not seen Jesus in the flesh, as the disciples did before the cross, nor in a "glorified body," as the first witnesses did during the seminal period.

In other important respects our experience relates closely to theirs and is informed and interpreted by theirs. We should remember that the church of Matthew and the other evangelists knew Jesus as Lord and knew him as present in their midst. To an extent, as we have noted, the evangelists may have narrated the seminal encounters with the Lord Jesus in the light of their own experience of Jesus as present in their midst. Such sayings as the benediction cited were addressed to the church of the first century, in which "seeing" the Lord was no longer possible.

Presence among Us in Word and Sacrament

The story of the appearance to the disciples at Emmaus is a particularly helpful case in point. It testifies to the presence of the Lord in "the breaking of bread" and as Scriptures were "opened." Christ was known to the first witnesses as he came into their midst, took bread, blessed it, broke it, and distributed it. As we have noted, several of the appearances seem to have involved a meal. He may have been recognized as the action and words of the Last Supper were remembered. Furthermore, the early church knew him as present—as he had promised he would be—when it gathered at table and broke bread in memory of him. Thus the Last Supper, the seminal encounters, and the eucharistic meal of the early church are brought into relationship in the story in Luke 24 (see pp. 63-68 herein).

It was also the experience of the first witnesses that he was known to them especially in the interpretation of Scripture. They said that he was the interpreter of Scripture and that Scripture (the Old Testament) made him known. This too was the experience of the first-century church. As Scripture was read and heard, exposited in preaching, meditated on, and prayed over, he was present to them in a real and special way.

He is present to us also in the breaking of bread and in the proclaiming and hearing of the scriptural word. Today these are the most important modes of his presence in the midst of the church assembled. We take seriously his promise that where two or three are gathered together in his name, he will be in their midst (Matt. 18:20). We take seriously his command to break bread in his memory as we gather in his name. He is present with us, but not in the sense in which he was present to the two on the way to Emmaus or to the twelve or to Paul in that brief and critical

period. He is present with us in the spirit as he promised to
the first witnesses: "I am with you always, to the close of the
age" (Matt. 28:20).

After that seminal period in which he appeared to his
followers, he left them as he said he would. After that, they
did not experience his presence again in the same mode as
they had earlier. The ascension narrative is a way of de-
marking the limits of the period of encounters with the re-
created Jesus as Lord. (The forty days seems both artificial
and at variance with the timing of Paul's experience, but in
any case, ascension is the name by which the church dis-
tinguishes the period of the appearances from the rest of
time, and for convenience I will use it here.)

The first witnesses (except for Paul) knew him before the
cross and after his death encountered him as Lord in a
"body of glory." After the ascension they knew him as present when they broke bread in his name and as the Scripture
was unfolded. This was in accord with his earlier promise to
them. They witnessed to his presence among them in one
mode before the ascension. The Emmaus narrative witnesses both to that and to their later experience of the presence of his spirit among them after the ascension.

We cannot "see" him. He is not present to us in a "body of
glory." But he is present to us in precisely the same sense as
he was present after the ascension to the apostolic witnesses
and to the first-century church. We are they who are
blessed because we have not seen and yet believe. We also
trust in the promise that he will be with us, not only because
the early witnesses have passed his promise on to us but,
more importantly, because we also have experienced his
presence. The Emmaus story rings true because our hearts
also burn within us as the Scripture is unfolded and because
he is known to us also in the breaking of the bread. Word
and sacrament remain the special marks of his presence in
the assembled church today. His presence in Word and
sacrament today is our link with the seminal encounters.

I am one of those sacramentally oriented Christians who
find it easy—perhaps too easy—to speak of the Lord Jesus

as being present when the church assembles to break bread in his name. We say he is "really" present, yet we lack a philosophical basis for defining the "real." We don't use "real" in this connection in the same way we use it to say that another human person standing next to us is "really" present. Few of us find either Platonic realism or Aristotelian realism viable alternatives, yet we know that the church's notion of his real presence has in the past been explained principally from the standpoint of Aristotle or Plato. Furthermore, we know, as did earlier Christians making use of Greek philosophical apologetics, that his presence is a mystery never to be fully rationalized. However, to say in our culture that something is a mystery is to risk being considered obscurantist. But a mystery it remains nonetheless.

Some will analyze his presence in our midst in terms of human feelings. We know him to be with us because we feel deeply moved. This is not to be dismissed too easily; we should note that this is how Luke relates Christ's presence: "Did not our hearts burn within us . . . while he opened to us the scriptures?" (24:32). Yet we do not wish to reduce his presence to our emotional response.

Since this is not a book on sacramental theology, I will not develop this point further. However, I should note that the presence today of the Re-created One, or the presence of the spirit of Jesus as Lord, is hard to grasp apart from some understanding of his real presence in Word and sacrament. One reason for our unease about the re-creation may be the relative unease that a large number of us feel in speaking about his real presence among us as we gather for worship.

Presence in the World

We know from our own experience and from the witness of the first Christians that the presence of Jesus as Lord was never confined to the assembled church alone. His promise to be with us until the close of the age is not limited to his presence as we assemble to break bread in his name or to hear the Word proclaimed, as important as that is. He sent the first witnesses into the world and promised to go with them and to empower them with his spirit. So also with us.

However, we do not possess an Easter narrative that will do for his worldly presence what the Emmaus narrative does for our understanding of his presence in Word and sacrament. We have less to go on, but there are hints. Matthew's Gospel is the Gospel of the promise: "Where two or three are gathered in my name, there am I in the midst of them" (18:20). It is also the Gospel containing the parable of the Last Judgment (25:31-46). In this parable the Son of Man comes in glory to judge the world, judging on the basis of who shows compassionate concern for his neighbor in need. The Son of Man—the King—says to those "blessed of my Father" that they will inherit the Father's kingdom, "for I was hungry and you gave me food, I was thirsty and you gave me drink, I was a stranger and you welcomed me, I was naked and you clothed me, I was sick and you visited me, I was in prison and you came to me" (vv. 35-36). The righteous demur, saying, "Lord, when did we see thee hungry and feed thee, or thirsty and give thee drink," and so forth (v. 37). And the King answers, "Truly, I say to you, as you did it to one of the least of these my brethren, you did it to me" (v. 40).

A possible interpretation is that Jesus as Christ so identifies himself with the hungry and sick and naked that he is present in the midst of the needy when we go to minister to them in his name. He is with the hungry, the sick, the poor, and so on. However, we should be careful about interpreting a parable too literally, while recognizing that the church has for centuries seen Christ in the neighbor in need.

As we have noted, the appearance narratives have an element of command that includes the requirement to forgive sins and, in John 21, to feed the sheep of Christ out of love for him. In the broadest sense, feeding or nurturing the sheep of Christ includes meeting their needs both physically and spiritually. Furthermore, forgiveness entails whatever is required to facilitate restoring people to a creative relationship with God and with one another.

We are commissioned to go into the world in his name as agents of forgiveness and as nurturers of the sheep of Christ. We are promised that he will be with us, and we expect to meet him in our brother and sister in need. It is not stretching the promise too far to use the word "presence" in this connection. He will be present with us till the close of the age, present in the neighbor in need. He is present as the forgiven forgive others. The shepherd is present as our love for him moves us to feed his sheep.

CHAPTER 9

The Pattern as Paradigm

In the previous chapter I have considered the presence of Jesus as Lord among the first witnesses and compared it with his presence among us. In the course of the discussion I have mentioned that the narratives are all marked by a pattern of presence, command, and promise, and I have commented on the relationship of these elements to each other. I have discussed what I have labeled "the faithful stance" of the apostolic witnesses—their response in worship, obedience, and trust.

Throughout the book I have described the pattern and occasionally alluded to its function as a paradigm for our understanding ourselves both as a worshiping body and as individuals. In this chapter I wish to draw out the implications of the paradigm. Let us begin by looking at the relationships among the several elements.

PRESENCE WITHOUT COMMAND: ADORATION WITHOUT OBEDIENCE

The apostolic witnesses saw him and worshiped him, experienced him as Lord and responded in adoration. But they did not stop there. They were not allowed to. For he had not come into their presence to remain there—in fact, he did not remain there. He was known as he was going away. They could not hold him. He would not remain at the table at Emmaus.

He was present to commission them, to send them out. As he was sent, so they were sent. He did not call them "to be with him," as he had in his earlier ministry (Mark 3:14). He came to them to empower them to go. They were to teach,

to make disciples, to preach, to forgive, to love, to baptize—
not to stay on a mountaintop or in an upper room.

The narratives are peripatetic, full of comings and
goings. Christ comes unannounced and unexpected, and
goes as he comes. His followers come together and are dis-
persed to all nations, to the ends of the earth.

In what way is this pattern a paradigm for us? First, as I
have suggested several times, the church and its people
can't stay on the mountaintop or in the upper room. We
can't cling to his feet. If we do, we will lose him.

Sacramentalism or pietism of any sort is a dead end. Religion that has as its aim conjuring up the Lord's presence
and basking in it will only end up losing him. His presence
can't be conjured up, and he can't be confined to the assembled community. The downfall of medieval sacramentalism did not occur because Jesus Christ was not in the
midst of the faithful at the mass, as some Protestants insis-
ted. It occurred because the church tried to domesticate the
Lord's presence, to bring him to his people on schedule, as
announced. It occurred because they bought and sold his
presence, which was more stupid than blasphemous, because anyone reading Scripture knows that the Lord cannot
be controlled by human caprice.

Sacramentalism at any time in history falls into the same
trap. It becomes an end in itself, the goal and purpose of
life. It loses all sense of mission. This is the particular trap of
my own church. Our sacramental heritage, with its great
beauty and rich poetry, becomes a substitute for doing the
will of God. It offers a refuge from the world, a permanent
hiding place.

Most sacramental churches, including the Church of
Rome and the Anglican Church, know that sacramental
piety that excludes mission is distorted and soon corrupt,
or, more likely, hollow and lifeless. The prophetic strain
acts as a corrective in many instances, so my pointing out a
tendency toward sacramentalism is not meant as an indict-
ment of a whole church.

Far more insidious today, in my judgment, are nonsacramental forms of pietism. Here also the goal of religion is to get into the presence of the Lord and stay there by withdrawing from the world. The Word replaces the sacrament as the idol, or sometimes the two are combined. Instead of being conjured up in the mass, Christ is conjured up in the Bible group or at the prayer meeting. The Emmaus road experience is sought over and over again. The flames in the heart are fanned through exhortation and technique by today's substitute for the mass priest—the mass evangelist. Prayer meetings every night and charismatic highs become the central purpose of living.

Why do I say this is more insidious than sacramental piety? Because sacramental piety is no longer commercialized, but biblicism is. Sacramentalism has had hundreds of years of reformation critique, while biblicism is relatively unscathed by comparison. But both are faulty and truncated forms of Christian expression. Hans W. Frei in *The Identity of Jesus Christ* comments in passing, "It is . . . notorious that ecclesiastical bodies characterized by sacramental or Biblicist traditionalism have found passionate commitment to the fulfillment of human hopes and aspirations in history a difficult thing."[1] Sacramentalism and biblicism and the piety that they foster are usually world-denying or at least uninterested in the world around them, particularly the world that differs substantially from their own (frequently middle-class) world. Rarely does such piety issue in fervor for joining Christ in the world, for finding him present among the least of his brothers and sisters. Both forms of piety issue from a fundamental misunderstanding of the nature of new life in Christ. Life with Jesus as Lord is not only found in the church. It is there, but it is also lived in obedience to his command to go forth in his name. Further, the full experience of the presence of the Lord is known in the process of carrying out his command to bring all nations into discipleship, with all that this entails.

1. Hans W. Frei, *The Identity of Jesus Christ: The Hermeneutical Bases of Dogmatic Theology* (Philadelphia: Fortress Press, 1975), p. 158.

Some obvious statements should be added. In his presence we know ourselves as forgiven, but we realize this fully only as we are instruments of forgiveness. In his presence we know his love, but we find fulfillment only as we feed his sheep. With him we are learners (disciples), but our learning is perfected only in teaching.

COMMAND WITHOUT PRESENCE: OBEDIENCE WITHOUT ADORATION

We cannot remain too long in Christ's presence without losing him, but if we eschew all piety we shall surely lose him. The teacher must also be a learner; the forgiver needs forgiveness; the feeder must be fed. Christian moral activists frequently deplore religious experience, whether of the sacramental or word-centered variety. They see the excess and too frequently disavow any need for the presence of the Lord in the assembly. They are rightly called into the world, but they wrongly turn away from time spent in his presence apart from the world. The apostolic witnesses knew awe in his presence; they knew holy fear; they were confronted by his majesty and overwhelmed by his authority. This encounter was the source of their missionary zeal and the corrective of their zealousness. So with us today.

Moral activism without holy quietism quickly becomes censorious and judgmental and eventually cynical. We all know "movement" Christians too long away from the altar and the book whose zealotry issues more from their inner obsessions than from the Lord's command to obedience. Work in the world in his name should issue from his presence if it is to reflect his compassion rather than only our passion. New life should be enjoyed to be shared; this means spending time away from the world in his presence in order that his presence might be made manifest in the world.

This is a special problem for the clergy. We are expected to be agents of forgiveness and frequently lose sight of our need to be forgiven. We are expected to show forth his love and frequently cut ourselves off from his love. We are expected to teach and frequently stop sitting at his feet as learners. We are expected to bring others into his presence and frequently do not allow ourselves enough time with him.

PRESENCE AND COMMAND WITHOUT PROMISE: ADORATION AND OBEDIENCE WITHOUT TRUST

The seminal experience as reflected in the appearance narratives includes a third and essential element, as we have seen. The apostolic witnesses heard a promise and went forth into the world with that promise ringing in their ears: "I am with you always, to the close of the age" (Matt. 28:20). The promise was alternatively understood by John and Luke as empowerment by the spirit, given them by Jesus the Lord himself. They understood that they could not remain long in his presence but that his spirit would go with them into the world. They trusted in his promise.

The element of trust is absolutely essential for the life of the Christian today. It is not all there is to the faithful stance (see pp. 88-89 herein), but it is an essential ingredient. Fulfilled life for the Christian—or life as a new creature— involves both life in the assembled community, where Jesus as Lord is known to be present in Word and sacrament, and going out into the world in obedience to his command. These elements must work together; when they are separated, distortions occur.

The promise and trust in it is the link between the two. If we people of the church are to live in the world and be obedient to the Lord's command, we must spend most of life outside of the assembled community. This is as it should be. The sacramentalist and biblicist "solution" is no solution. We are meant to live in the world, to live in obedience to his command. Most of the time, therefore, we are living away from his special presence in Word and sacrament. But

we are not totally apart from his presence, for he has promised to be with us and has breathed his spirit upon us, empowering us to go out in his name.

The word that characterizes our response to his promise
is "trust." We go out into the world in obedience, trying to
carry out his command, trusting that he will be with us. We
experience high points of his presence in the gathered community when "our hearts burn within us," but we know
these moments are few and far between. Though these
moments are central and essential, we do not live life solely
to bring about these special times.

Fortunately, life outside is not life apart from his presence. We may have little psychic or emotional evidence of
his presence, but we trust he is present. We have known his
presence in Word and sacrament, and will again. We have
known his presence in those to whom we go in his name—
the hungry, the naked, the sick—and we will again. But
most of life is lived in between these moments, and it must
be lived in trust, trust that he goes with us as he promised.

Trust that he is with us is sustained both by the memory
of the special and sacred moments of his presence and by
prayer. The memory motivates prayer, and the prayer
stimulates memory. Being with another person in a deep
and productive sense, face to face or soul to soul, requires
dialogue. Dialogue between people deepens the "withness"
of our mutual presence one with another. Furthermore,
this dialogue creates and sustains trust. Obviously, this does
not characterize all human relationships; many are casual,
and some are destructive. But when there is caring, dialogue encourages trust.

Prayer is the form of dialogue that sustains and encourages trust in his promise. We know he is present as we go out
from the special moments of his sacred presence. The fatal-
ist says to his departing friend, "Good luck." Unfortunately,
we Christians more often than not use the language of fatal-
ism, too. But we should remember Christ's promise—"I am
with you always"—and say, "Go with God." "God be with
you" is the true meaning of "Good-bye," and that is not only

the appropriate word for departing friends but a sign of
our memory of the promise and of our trust in it. The
French and the Spanish commit their friends to God's care
with "Adieu" and "Adios."

Prayer—as dialogue with the Lord Jesus, who promises
to be with us—reminds us that he is indeed with us. Like the
best of human language, prayer functions to deepen trust,
to sharpen the sense of "withness." We know, emotionally
and intellectually, the difference between the sacred moments of his real presence with us in the midst of the people
of God and his presence with us as we are alone on the road.
Trust, sustained by prayer, brings his promise to life.

Thousands of volumes have been written on prayer
and perhaps hundreds on God's presence since Brother
Lawrence's writings were collected in *The Practice of the Presence of God* in the late seventeenth century. This is not the
place (and I am not the author) to add significantly to that
corpus. What I will add is a small personal note. Trust in the
promise is what sustains me personally. When I bring that
promise to mind, I know he is with me. Though by vocation
and ministry I live much of my life in the sacred moments,
the spaces in between the high places of his presence are
vast. Remembering the promise and trusting in it makes life
outside possible, and more fulfilling.

Furthermore, I am reminded that the promise "I am
with you always" sustained Moses and Jeremiah, and I am
sure it sustained the apostolic witnesses. We are in a tradition with a "cloud of witnesses" who have trusted in that
promise, and that encourages me also. I do not trust only
because they trusted, but their lives demonstrate that the
promise can be trusted, and my experience confirms it.

Trust is the link in several ways. We trust Christ is present
with us even when he seems absent. We have known his
presence and heard his promise, and we trust it even when
experience appears to deny it. In addition, trust in the
promise of his presence provides a link between the time of
his sacred presence and the time, the greater time, of faith-

ful obedience to enacting his command in the world. Obedience is an act of the will in response to his command. This willing act is carried out in a climate of trust that he will be with us as we go where obedience leads us to do what obedience calls for.

Thus adoration as a response to his presence, obedience as a response to his command, and trust as a response to his promise are essentially related. Together they comprised the response of the apostolic witnesses to their encounter with him. I have described this constellation of adoration, obedience, and trust as the faithful stance or response of the earliest Christians (see pp. 88-89 herein). So also with us. What I have said about their faith is meant to apply to us as well. Faith is not only adoration, not only obedience, not only trust. The faithful stance involves all three, inextricably intertwined with trust, which I believe is the linchpin that holds them together.

RE-CREATION AND LIFE AFTER DEATH

The paradigm is much more functional for understanding the faithful stance in this life than in the next. It arises from traditions that have their roots in the seminal encounter. That encounter involved Jesus re-created as Lord. As the "firstborn" of the new creation, as the "second Adam," he bridges the two creations. The appearances occur in history in this or the first creation, though God's act of re-creation ("raising" Jesus from the dead) is beyond history. For a brief period—the time between his death on the cross and the ascension (see p. 92 herein)—Jesus as Lord, re-created by the Father, appeared to his followers. In their encounter with him they got a "glimpse" of the new creation and participated with him in it.

They heard his promise that he would be with them always, until the end of the age (Matt. 28:20). Most probably this means that his spirit will be with his followers until the present order comes to an end. However, "always" may suggest that the promise extends to the next age.

When we try to speak (or write) of life beyond death (or life beyond this life), we necessarily engage in speculation. We have the benefit of Paul's speculation, which is very important, but it too is speculation, as the language of 1 Corinthians 15 clearly shows. Paul had met the Lord Jesus in a "glorified body," and he firmly believed that he, with a similar body, would participate in the new order of creation together with Jesus.

For me, the heart of Paul's case for the re-creation of all believers has its roots in his Epistle to the Romans. There he argues (8:35-39) that nothing, absolutely nothing—not even death—"will be able to separate us from the love of God in Christ Jesus our Lord" (v. 39). He had participated in that love beginning with his encounter on the Damascus road. As "love never ends" (1 Cor. 13:8) in the relationship between Paul and the Lord Jesus Christ (as Paul usually refers to him), so the relationship that is characterized and constituted by love can never end. That relationship begun in a blinding light culminates, so Paul speculates, "face to face" (1 Cor. 13:12).

It is unthinkable for Paul, and for me, that the relationship with Jesus as Lord, begun in history, in this life, should ever end. It must survive this life and therefore survive death—hence the promise of his presence becomes "I am with you always, to the close of the age" *and beyond.* This may be what the Eastern church means to suggest in the ending of all its benedictions—"now and ever and unto ages of ages." ("The blessing of the Lord be upon you through his grace and love for mankind always, now and ever and unto ages of ages.") It is clearly what the Eastern church means by the words exchanged by the officiating priests at the Peace: "Christ is in our midst. He is and shall be." He was present to the apostolic witnesses, he is present in spirit now to us, and he will be present with us in the age to come.

We have briefly reviewed Paul's speculation about the

resurrection of all believers (see pp. 16-18 herein). The Corinthian Christians, apparently accepting the re-creation of Jesus as Lord, questioned whether they would participate in the resurrection of the dead. Paul argues that the two are necessarily related: "Now if Christ is preached as raised from the dead, how can some of you say that there is no resurrection of the dead? But if there is no resurrection of the dead, then Christ has not been raised; if Christ has not been raised, then our preaching is in vain and your faith is in vain" (1 Cor. 15:12-14).

The Corinthians have asked further questions: "How are the dead raised? With what kind of body do they come?" (1 Cor. 15:35). Paul castigates them: "You foolish man!" (v. 36). As I have said earlier, the question does not appear foolish to me; we are still asking it. In any event, Paul is convinced that we will be re-created as Jesus has been and will be given a body like his: "But our commonwealth is in heaven, and from it we await a Savior, the Lord Jesus Christ, who will change our lowly body to be like his glorious body, by the power which enables him even to subject all things to himself" (Phil. 3:20-21). Paul speculates, probably on the basis of his experience of Jesus as Lord on the Damascus road, that this body that will be given us will be glorious, spiritual, and imperishable, like that of Jesus. Further, as there was continuity of person between Jesus of Nazareth and Jesus as Lord, between the crucified and the re-created, so with us there will be continuity. We will maintain our personal identities, though there will be discontinuity between our earthly bodies, destined for death, and our glorified bodies, destined for life eternal.

Speculation about life beyond this one bothers me. In the Middle Ages the Latin mind was driven to all manner of speculation, which led inevitably to imaginings of purgatory and a multiplicity of heavens and hells. I prefer to control my curiosity and limit my conclusions to that about which I am more certain. On this basis I have reached five conclusions.

First, we know and experience the presence of Jesus as Lord. We can say "He is in our midst!" (which is a response in the eucharistic liturgy of my church).

Second, we trust in his promise that he will be with us always.

Third, like Paul, I find it unthinkable that my death could separate me from his presence or his love.

Fourth, as a consequence of this trust and this conviction, I believe that by God's power I will be enabled after death to be in relationship with Jesus, whom I now know as Lord.

Fifth, this ultimate relationship will require some vehicle for personal communication. Paul calls it a "glorified body" or a "spiritual body." Like Paul, I know of no other means by which an individual can communicate except through a body, so his speculation seems sensible. Furthermore, when he and the apostolic witnesses were in communication with Jesus present in their midst, Jesus was apparently in a re-created body. Paul insists that our new bodies will "be like his glorious body." I accept his conclusion and feel no need to go beyond it. I say with conviction the profession in the Apostles' Creed, "I believe in . . . the resurrection of the *body*," which I understand in this way. However, I prefer the profession in the Nicene Creed: "I look for the resurrection of the *dead*." The latter is more ambiguous and leaves open the means by which we will communicate. The narratives we have been considering can take us no further, and I do not wish to go any farther afield.

Having said this, I should note what I have not said. Life beyond this one requires a new act of creation like the one that began it all. We believe this is possible because we believe the new creation to have been initiated in the re-creation of Jesus as Lord. Our participation in life after death will be the result of a creative act of God that will enable us to continue the relationship with Jesus Christ begun in this life. This is *not* the same as belief in an "eternal soul." There is no such belief entailed by the re-creation. The concept of an eternal soul is a pre-Christian Greek idea, often mistakenly mixed with Christian belief in the re-creation. Furthermore, re-creation is not to be confused with reincarnation, which is an Eastern belief with no connection to Christianity at all. Re-creation is not resuscitation. Our body dies and decays and returns to the elements, "ashes to ashes and dust to dust."

Without the re-creation of Jesus our Lord, this life is all there is, the end. There is no other warrant for belief in any existence beyond this one apart from the conviction that God has raised Jesus from the dead, that Jesus our Lord is "the first-born among many brethren" (Rom. 8:29). Without the re-creation of Jesus as Lord, there is no reason I can find for hope in life beyond this life, just as there is no basis for the rest of the Christian enterprise. It all hinges on this one mighty act of God to which the apostolic witnesses testify and in which I firmly believe.

RE-CREATION AND NEW LIFE HERE AND NOW—A PERSONAL POSTSCRIPT

Believing in the re-creation is not intellectual assent to the proposition that Jesus was raised from the dead. Though our intellect must be engaged, much more is involved. Nor is such belief a historical conclusion about a past event, though historical analysis is involved, as I have noted. Nor is it only belief about the future beyond this age, though that is important.

When I say "Christ is risen" or "Jesus is Lord," I am not making a historical observation or stating a proposition, though the words and the form do appear propositional, and they certainly involve our history. When I make such a statement, I am proclaiming my stance toward life and identifying myself with a particular view of the world and its history. It is really a very complex statement. Let me explain.

For me to say "Christ is risen" is to say that I wish to be understood as standing within the tradition of the first witnesses. I am identifying myself with their stance toward

Jesus, whom they encountered as Lord. I am saying that
Jesus is in the midst of the Christian community as Lord
and that I have encountered him there. In Word and sacrament I have met him; in sacred moments he has been present, bringing joy and fear and perplexity. Doubt has been a
part of my experience, doubt that the Lord was present and
doubt that the Lord was to be understood in the light of the
cross. Both emotion and intellect have been engaged.

But this is not all. I have come to understand this experience in the light of a particular and peculiar history, a history to which the New Testament bears witness. This history
focuses on a strange series of events that we refer to as
Easter and that this book is all about. I am not detached
from this history; I see myself as participating in it. It is all
about my past and my present and my future, and each
Sunday I celebrate it and make it new and fresh.

But I do not live my life—at least not most of it—in adoration of Jesus who is present as Lord. I do not devote most of
my waking hours to seeking the presence of the Lord.
Rather, I am more aware of having been commissioned,
called, ordered, commanded to live life in a certain way,
which I have called obedience. To say "Christ is risen" or
"Jesus is Lord" is to hear and obey a command. Obedience
is unfashionable, but this is what is involved. However, this
commission is not a childish call to be a good boy. It is a
command to share this stance toward life with others, to
make disciples, to teach and heal, to be his agent of forgiveness and love in the world. I am one under authority. I may
resist the command—and I do, particularly when it is incon-
venient or threatens my tranquility—but like a member of
the armed forces, I am under authority until I muster out.

Obedience takes me to places I would not go and to people I would not choose, and links me to causes I might not
join. Obedience upsets my middle-class values. Obedience
makes me feel guilty, while the therapeutic world around
me labels all guilt as "wrong feelings."

The stance of fidelity to Jesus who is Lord involves the
will, of course, but like all true loyalty, something outside of

me calls it forth. Christ risen, or the Lord Jesus who is present, evokes my obedience, calls forth my loyalty as would a loyal friend or an admirable leader—not a tyrant. I am loyal—or at least I try to be—because I want to be, not because I have to be.

I want to be faithful because he is faithful to me. He does not send me out alone. Like the best of leaders, he goes before me. Not that I am always aware of it at the time, but I go hoping to meet him, hoping to join him. I live in a badly divided, distorted world bent on destroying itself, a world divided into tribes, with nation against nation, race against race, class against class, and sex against sex. My nation is the most powerful in the world, and my race and my sex are the most powerful in the United States, and it would be comfortable just to enjoy that position of superiority. However, my loyalty to his Word tells me that this is not as it should be and not as it will be. My fidelity tells me that I must be doing something to change this even against my personal interest. I could not or would not do anything of the sort unless I knew he was with me in the struggle.

All this involves not simply the will to obey but a large measure of trust in his promise, a promise to be with us not only in the sacred places and sacred moments but in the world where he has commanded us to go. I have said much about this promise to be with us because it explains how I live and because it has been neglected in many considerations of the meaning of new life.

Living by the promise of his presence helps me to remain loyal (faithful) even when he seems absent. Trusting in the promise of his presence saves me from perpetual involvement in a frantic search for his presence. I don't have to go to mass each morning or to a prayer meeting each evening. I don't need to search him out. He is with me as he has promised, even when his presence is not evident to my senses.

This stance of fidelity, usually called faith, is a response to the initiative of Jesus the Lord. He is present. I have known him in our midst. I have responded on my knees. He has commanded me. I have heard his voice through Scripture and through prophets, both ancient and contemporary. I have tried to live in obedience. He has promised me his supportive presence. I have heard his promise, and I trust in it. He has kept his word even though I have not kept mine.

This is what I know to be faith. It is social, because I am part of a faithful community, but also personal, because I must make my own commitments as well. It is intellectual; it requires strenuous thought because the world's intellectual bias, which is also part of my mind-set, is against such faith. It is moral, and it involves the will; I am frequently called on to will what a narcissistic world calls "folly." It is emotional, sometimes soaring high as the cathedral vaulting, sometimes not. It is fun—yes, fun! In a rather grim age, the stance of faith involves surprise and folly and enthusiasm—the real kind—brought about by his presence in us. And that is fun!

This taste of the new creation is rich fare, very rich indeed. Who knows what to expect when it arrives fully, and we see him face to face.

Appendix 1

Wolfhart Pannenberg's Case for the Resurrection as a Historic Event

Pannenberg examines the historical evidence of the Resurrection (as we have done throughout this book). His case for the reasonable probability of the appearances of Jesus as historic rests first and foremost on the Pauline witness in 1 Corinthians 15:3-8. Paul, writing in approximately A.D. 55 or perhaps twenty-five years after the crucifixion, claims that the Lord "appeared" to him (or "was seen" by him). (Pannenberg concludes from Gal. 1:18 that Paul's conversion may have been during the period A.D. 33-35, or three to five years after the crucifixion.)[1] Paul is the only eyewitness to write of an appearance, and this letter is the earliest written account of the appearances, coming perhaps fifteen years before Mark's Gospel and perhaps two generations before the fourth Gospel.

Furthermore, Paul believed that "he had been granted an appearance of the same sort as the other apostles before him."[2] The letter cites, without elaboration, appearances to Peter, to the twelve, to five hundred brethren, to James, and to all the apostles. Paul is writing to the Corinthians as if this were common knowledge, and indeed, since many of the witnesses would have been alive at the time, Paul's report would have been verifiable within the early Christian

---

1. Pannenberg, *Jesus—God and Man* (Philadelphia: Westminster Press, 1968), p. 90.
2. Pannenberg, *Jesus—God and Man*, p. 77. Others agree with this conclusion. See pp. 11-12.

community. Pannenberg therefore concludes that "in view
of the age of the formulated traditions used by Paul and of
the proximity of Paul to the events, the assumption that
appearances of the resurrected Lord were really experienced by a number of members of the primitive Christian
community and not perhaps freely invented in the course
of later legendary development has good historical foundation."[3] Other narratives of the appearances circulated independently of Paul, and though they were found in written
form years after his letter to Corinth, it is probable that they
reflect experiences that took place earlier.

It could be, of course, that these experiences, including
Paul's, were purely subjective hallucinations. But Pannenberg believes, as I do, that the number of such reports and
their distribution over time and space makes such a conclusion unlikely.[4] Also, the view that the appearances were
hallucinations does not account well for the subsequent behavior of the apostles. They were prepared to die for a faith
grounded in belief in Jesus' re-creation.

Pannenberg claims further that the resurrection is not
impossible from a scientific point of view and that contemporary understanding of natural "laws" precludes firm
pronouncements about the occurrence of an individual
event: "Natural science expresses the general validity of the
laws of nature but must at the same time declare its own
inability to make definitive judgments about the possibility
or impossibility of an individual event, regardless of how
certainly it is able, at least in principle, to measure the probability of an event's occurrence."[5] Though his argument is
lengthy and somewhat tortuous,[6] I agree with his conclusion, as I think would Walter Kunneth. Contemporary scientific understanding of the natural order cannot rule out

3. Pannenberg, *Jesus—God and Man*, p. 91.
4. Pannenberg, *Jesus—God and Man*, pp. 96ff.
5. Pannenberg, *Jesus—God and Man*, p. 98.
6. For a helpful discussion of Pannenberg's argument, see David
McKenzie, *Wolfhart Pannenberg and Religious Philosophy* (Washington:
University Press of America, 1980), pp. 44-48.

the occurrence of a unique event—any event, not even the re-creation of Jesus.

Pannenberg also argues that the resurrection should not be excluded from the domain of events investigated by historians. He objects to what he calls "the principle of analogy," which is "the idea that every event of all times and places must be seen as just another instance of some type of event with which we are already familiar."[7] Applying this argument to the resurrection, Pannenberg asks,

> Does not the postulate of the fundamental homogeneity of all events usually form the chief argument against the historicity of the Resurrection of Jesus? But if that is so, does not the opinion, which has come to be regarded as virtually self-evident, that the Resurrection of Jesus cannot be a historical event, rest on a remarkably weak foundation? Only the particular characteristics of the reports about it make it possible to judge the historicity of the Resurrection, not the prejudgment that every event must be fundamentally of the same kind as every other.[8]

The problem, of course, is that we Christians assert that the re-creation is an act of God, an assertion that historians cannot rule out, but neither can they investigate it. David McKenzie, a careful commentator on the works of Pannenberg, reaches the following conclusion about Pannenberg's argument in his book *Wolfhart Pannenberg and Religious Philosophy*. Postulating the resurrection as an explanation for the emergence of early Christianity (which we do, of course) is not something ruled out by the current methodology of critical historiography, but neither is it provable by such methodology. Historians may investigate the facts surrounding the event; they may even conclude as individuals that the explanation of the church is plausible. However, because the resurrection requires a further defense of the

7. McKenzie, *Wolfhart Pannenberg and Religious Philosophy*, p. 89.
8. Pannenberg, *Redemption Event and History*, quoted in McKenzie, *Wolfhart Pannenberg and Religious Philosophy*, pp. 90-91.

existence of a God who acts in history, it is not likely to be supported by historians acting as historians.[9]

I agree with McKenzie's overall conclusions that Pannenberg has successfully removed some roadblocks to acknowledging the events surrounding the re-creation as historical. Too many nineteenth- and twentieth-century theologians (and biblical scholars) have uncritically accepted the view that the natural and historical sciences necessarily rule out the traditional interpretations of the re-creation. Like Kunneth, Pannenberg argues successfully that these sciences do not exclude the church's traditional explanation. However, Pannenberg's program goes further. He wants contemporary critical historians *outside the church* to accept his arguments that the re-creation is at least a plausible explanation for the existence of the church. Like McKenzie and other commentators, I don't think Pannenberg has effectively made that case.[10]

What kind of evidence would lead an impartial historian to the conclusion that the re-creation *as an act of God* is a plausible explanation for the existence of the church or for the about-face in the lives of the apostolic witnesses? The participation of God as the sole cause of the re-creation of Jesus is certainly outside of the realm of historical reason. However, historical reasoning can lead one to the conclusion that what happened demands an explanation and that the explanation put forward by Paul and the other early witnesses can be held as a credible alternative.

J. A. T. Robinson has argued that there could be certain historical facts incompatible with belief in the re-creation (see p. 3 herein). Also, there could conceivably be scientific theories that would be incompatible with belief in the re-creation (a completely closed mechanistic and deterministic system, for example). Such conclusions are abhorrent to theological positivists such as Karl Barth, who believe that the re-creation can be known only by faith totally apart

9. McKenzie, *Wolfhart Pannenberg and Religious Philosophy*, pp. 93-95.
10. For another appraisal of Pannenberg, see *Theology as History*, ed. James M. Robinson and John B. Cobb, vol. 3 of New Frontiers in Theology (New York: Harper & Row, 1967).

from historical reasoning, and therefore cannot be threatened by either history or science.

I don't believe it is necessary to side either with the theological positivist who argues from revelation alone, or with Pannenberg, who attempts to argue from reason alone. In *Easter Faith and History*, Daniel P. Fuller examines these positions and puts the alternatives this way: "Can the resurrection of Jesus stand by itself as an historical fact known through the historical method and thus provide a basis for faith, or in order to have Easter faith must one somehow receive the will to believe the resurrection as set forth in the New Testament without needing support from historical reason?"[11] Fuller puts Pannenberg at one pole, Barth at the other, and Richard Niebuhr in the middle with others who argue for the necessity of both reason and revelation and of both historical investigation and faith. Niebuhr has written the classical review of the history of the alternatives in a book entitled *Resurrection and Historical Reason,* published in 1957 (prior to most of the writings cited above). Having reviewed the works of Barth, Rudolf Bultmann, and the American theologian John Knox, Niebuhr notes that, despite their diversity, at least two of them agree on each of the following theses:

> 1) The historical Jesus Christ cannot be understood from a general or neutral point of view, but only from a specific, historical standpoint, the Christian community. 2) The medium of this indispensable relationship is the memory of the early church preserved and interpreted in the New Testament by that church itself. . . . 3) The memory of the resurrection is integral to the entire memory of the man Jesus. . . . Jesus gains his intelligibility from the resurrection encounters. 4) . . . The memory of the resurrection is fundamental to the community's understanding of its own present situation and experience.[12]

11. Fuller, *Easter Faith and History* (Grand Rapids: Eerdmans, 1965), p. 25.
12. Niebuhr, *Resurrection and Historical Reason: A Study of Theological Method* (New York: Scribner's, 1957), p. 103.

Niebuhr sees clearly that faith is grounded in neither historical reasoning alone nor the will to believe without support of historical reason. The person and re-creation of
Jesus Christ are understood in historic concreteness only
from within the church, which preserves and interprets the
memory of the early church set forth in the New Testament. Furthermore, the memory of the re-creation is integral to understanding Jesus Christ and to the self-
understanding of the present church.

Appendix 2

Four Sermons Preached in Washington Cathedral

CHRISTMAS EVE 1984

"God with Us"

"'Behold, a virgin shall conceive and bear a son, and his name shall be called Emmanuel' (which means, God with us)."

The good news of Christmas is that God is with us. The one whose birth we celebrate this night has a name. According to Matthew this Jesus, born of Mary, is to be known as Emmanuel. That is his name—Emmanuel—which means "God with us." We are this night celebrating the coming close of God, whose love for us moves him to be with us.

We have just sung,

Veiled in flesh the Godhead see;
Hail th' Incarnate Deity,
Pleased as man with men to dwell;
Jesus, our Emmanuel.

We have heard and sung these words so often—in hymns, in the *Messiah,* and in the Christmas story. We have seen the name Emmanuel on countless churches. We are so used to it that we have forgotten that it is a startling proclamation. For most people, after all, God is not with us; he is remote. He·is not with us; he is alien—he dwells in high and lofty places, unconcerned about the everyday affairs of mere humanity. This view has been prevalent for a long time. The eighteenth-century founders of our nation made little of Christmas. The remaining Puritans at the time were afraid of a Popish celebration that centered on the Blessed Virgin Mary, but your typical colonial leader was a Deist. He believed in a far-off God, a remote creator-clockmaker who created the machine that we know as our world, wound it up, and let it go. God was Providence with a capital "P," but he was not—definitely not—Emmanuel or "God with us."

Many today share this view; perhaps many of you do. Many can make little sense of the Christmas proclamation that God, the creator of the universe, is also God with us. Is the Christmas proclamation a problem for you? It is far out. What can we mean by it?

We know what it is to say that a friend, our parent, our child, or our husband or wife is with us. We rejoice this time of year especially when those absent from us come to be with us for the holidays. We know also that being with someone is not only a matter of physical proximity. For many are the times when we share a space, even a small space, with someone, even a member of our family, and they are not *really* with us. They are "far off," we say. To be with someone in the sense that counts is to share intimacy, to be in dialogue, to experience someone's care for us and to extend our care to him or her. We all know what it means to be with someone in a caring way, the "withness" that really counts.

Well, that is what we witness to when we say that Jesus is our Emmanuel; he who comes this night is with us in the close and personal sense of the word. The words "care" and "love," words that describe the best of human relationships, belong to the relationship between us and the God revealed as Emmanuel.

Jesus, who is called Emmanuel, showed—by his life and teaching, by his acts and words—what it means to be with us. He expressed both a passion for justice and a depth of love previously unknown. He taught us what "being with" really means: to be with not only those who love us but also with those whom no one loves. He was with the outcast as well as the upper caste, the sick as well as the healthy, and the weak as well as the strong.

He was with the people as one with special authority, yet he was not authoritarian. He was with people as one who ruled, but he was concerned lest he injure a bruised reed or quench a dimly burning flame. In him justice was tempered by mercy, love by justice.

He cared about the least of those he called his brothers and sisters: the hungry, the homeless, and those in prison. So close was he to them that he said we will find him there when we go to the least of our brothers and sisters and share ourselves with them. Inasmuch as we care for the least of these, his brothers and sisters, we care for him, he said. He is with the needy and meets us there when we share his love with his brethren in need.

His desire to be with the "wrong" sort of people, his extraordinary love for all sorts of men and women in all kinds of conditions, led to envy within the religious establishment. He cared for those the righteous avoided and ate with those they called sinners and broke the religious rules in order to heal the sick, both physically and spiritually.

He was with his people in the most complete sense of the word, and being with his people led to his death. The depth of his caring was a judgment on the religion of rectitude without love. The religiously righteous hated him and did away with him. (His care for the outcast is not too popular with moralists even in our day.) He could have chosen to live, but he chose instead to give himself as an offering for others. He loved life; he loved celebrations and parties so much that the pious called him a glutton and a drunkard. But he was willing to relinquish his life rather than be separated from those for whom he came.

So his coming to be with us was an enigma. "He came to his own," John tells us, and they "received him not." He came to the religious community to show it what it means for God to be with his people. They preferred to keep God at a distance and hung him on a cross. Emmanuel was too close to the comfortable for their comfort.

So also his coming to be with us sets up a similar tension. God who is remote is less of a worry. We can go our own way without a care—for others, that is. God who is remote leaves us alone to put ourselves first, to give priority to our family, our race, our gender, and our nation. God who is with us wants us to go with him into the remote corners of his world, to places we would prefer not to go. He who is with us woos us to follow him. To be with him is to be with others in his name. This is not always convenient. So we shouldn't censure the righteous Puritans of his day, because we know what it means to allow God to come too close.

Jesus, born of Mary and called Emmanuel, died at the hands of cynics who decided that they would prefer God to be kept at a distance. They killed him rather than allow him to be with them. They preferred their own company to his. They preferred their own company to that of the motley crew who followed Jesus, and they killed him because he came too close.

But he had promised his followers that where two or three would gather together in his name, he would be there, would be with them in their midst. The promise seemed empty to them after his death on the cross as they gathered for a meal, perhaps in his memory. He had died, and they thought he would no longer be with them. Yet into their disconsolate company he came. They were stunned. They testified that he lived. They testified that Jesus, who had been crucified, lived and was Lord. They testified that he was indeed with them, as he had promised he would be. They said he was with them as the Scripture was read and unfolded: "Did not our hearts burn within us . . . while he opened to us the scriptures?" They knew he was with them in the "breaking of bread." As they took bread, gave thanks, broke it, and distributed it in his name, he was present. The discouraged band of followers rushed out into an uncomprehending world proclaiming, He is risen; he is with us. Jesus is our Emmanuel.

This was their experience, and it can be yours. For he is present with us tonight as he promised—when believers break bread in his name, as we do here. He is with us tonight—as he promised—as we hear in the Scriptures the things concerning him. He will be with us as we go out in his name to his sisters and brothers in need.

He is with us in the most personal sense of that word. God came close in that Bethlehem stable, and he comes to us tonight. But he will not violate our integrity. He comes to the door only if we knock, comes into our lives only if we receive him. Those who love us will not violate our personhood; neither will he.

My friends, he is present with us this night. Hear the Christmas hymn and make it yours:

O holy Child of Bethlehem!
  Descend to us, we pray;
Cast out our sin and enter in,
  Be born in us today.
We hear the Christmas angels
  The great glad tidings tell;
O come to us, abide with us,
  Our Lord Emmanuel!

Hear his promise and trust in it—"I am with you always, to the close of the age." O come to us, abide with us, our Lord Emmanuel!

EASTER SUNDAY 1985

Mark 16:1-8

Hear, once again, the closing words of Mark's Gospel: "And they went out and fled from the tomb; for trembling and astonishment had come upon them; and they said nothing to any one, for they were afraid."

What a letdown! Mark begins his Gospel with the announcement "The beginning of the gospel of Jesus Christ, the Son of God," and he ends, "They said nothing to any one, for they were afraid." In eight verses the evangelist completes his Gospel with the tale of the women at the tomb, an abrupt ending—and, for many, an unsatisfactory one.

Your Bible at home may have twelve more verses in chapter 16, but most New Testament scholars accept the evidence that the oldest manuscripts ended at verse eight—where our reading today ended—on an ambiguous and enigmatic note. Some believe that Mark wrote a more complete ending that is now lost; others believe that he intended to end his Gospel at verse eight.

As it is, we find in Mark no account of the appearance of the Risen Lord, no gathering of the disciples in his presence—only fear and wonder and silence.

Let's take it as it is, though we know and treasure the other Easter stories: those of the appearance to Mary in the garden, the disciples on the road to Emmaus, the miraculous catch of fish, doubting Thomas, and above all, the several accounts of his presence among the disciples assembled together in one place. Let's think of ourselves as Christians in Mark's community—Greek-speaking, perhaps living in Rome, probably after the fall of the temple. Mark's Gospel is all we have. Can we consider this apparently inconclusive story to be good news? Can we possibly view the fear and the silence as good news? Can Mark have chosen to end on that note, and if so, what can he have meant by it?

To begin with, note that the three women must have told someone what happened at the tomb, or there would not be any such story at all. So perhaps Mark ended the Gospel the way he did to make a point. As we know from the rest of the Gospel, Mark knew and believed that Jesus is the Christ, the Son of God. Perhaps he realized that this truth cannot be proved. Writing almost forty years after the crucifixion, the author probably didn't arrive at his conviction that Christ lives by seeing the Risen Lord. And neither do we.

Mark knew, I believe, that faith in Jesus as the Christ is filled with ambiguity and doubt and is arrived at in fear and trembling. Perhaps he meant his Gospel to be open-ended, to offer us the opportunity to write ourselves into the story. In this sense Mark's Gospel can be seen as quite modern, though obviously it is a creature of the ancient world.

The ending as it is forces us to think about Mark's whole

narrative, with its breathless immediacy and its excruciating death scene. Jesus, the Rabbi of such promise, dies. The vigorous young leader willingly goes to his death, his ministry apparently at an end. He is buried in a borrowed tomb. It is all over and done. He is dead and gone. His leadership is finished. He belongs to the past. Is that where the story ends for you? A brief and captivating episode in history, attractive but over. That is what the three women thought. They came as soon as they could after the Sabbath prohibition to anoint his dead body, to do the last responsible thing they could for him.

But they were surprised. The tomb was empty. They were greeted by a young man with an astounding message: "Do not be amazed; you seek Jesus of Nazareth, who was crucified. He has risen, he is not here."

He does not belong to the past. Don't look for him in a tomb. Don't seek him among the dead pages of the past. He is not there. Jesus who was crucified belongs not to the past but to the present and the future.

Death is real. It is the driving force of this world. Violence and destruction surround us. Our world is fascinated with death: the gun and the bomb are its symbols and totems. Our world is dying—it is entropic, winding down. And it belongs to the past.

Jesus, whom we perceive to be the Christ, is not to be found in the tomb. He is not part of the death of this world. He lives. He is a new creation, the real meaning of the words "he has risen." He represents the rejection of death as a way of life. A smoking gun does not make his day. Nor does a nuclear missile. They belong to death and the past, to the old, decaying civilization. He is the future. He is not in the tomb.

There is a second part to the young man's message. He tells the three faithful women that "he (Jesus) is going before you." He is the future, and he leads us into it. He goes before us! We follow him into the future; we do not seek after the status quo. His is a dynamic cause, not a static one. Life over death, future over past, movement over inertia.

He goes before us, calling us, urging us, wooing us, mov-

ing on, not standing still. This is why we Christians are often
dissatisfied with what is. We want to go where he goes and to
be where he is, not entombed in some frozen past but looking forward to and working toward a future with hope.

There is a third part to the message of the young man:
"Go and tell!" Don't keep this news to yourself. "Go and
tell." Go, tell it on the mountain. Don't be passive. Don't be
silent. That is to give in to death, to be doomed to the dead
past. Go and tell that he lives and that he goes before us. Go
and tell that he is a new creature and that we too are meant
for new life rather than for the old and all-too-familiar
death.

Life rules, not death. The future beckons, not the dead
hand of the past. Follow; don't stand still. Go and tell; don't
remain silent.

What a message! No wonder the women fled in fear; no
wonder they were awestruck. This is an astonishing revelation. If it doesn't seem so to you, maybe you have missed the
point of Mark's terse report.

The young man wanted the women to break with the
past, to leave the tomb, to abandon their preoccupation
with death. He wanted them to believe that this world of
death does not control us totally, that the tomb is not the
end.

For me, the young man in white is the church, the bearer
of the good news, a pointer to the future. Though he speaks
from the tomb, he looks beyond death. Though he reminds
us of the cross, he looks toward life. He is the voice that
directs us away from what drags us back and toward what
moves us forward.

He offers us a choice. Death or life, past or future. Dynamic motion or status quo.

Like the women at the tomb, we must decide. Fear and
trembling is appropriate. The dead past has a powerful
grip on us. The quest for security and power and comfort
has a mighty hold on us. It is a fearful thing to shake it loose.

And do we really know that he lives and that he goes
before us? We want proof. We want more than a report

from a few women at a tomb. But that is all Mark is prepared to offer, for there is no final proof. There is the
church with all its ambiguities and all its imperfections.
There is the community of the faithful, a mixture of both
the good and the bad. There are the sacraments. One we
celebrate today: the Eucharist or Holy Communion or
Mass—ignored by some, profaned by some, sometimes sur-
rounded by superstition. Yet somehow in this mixed company—the church—and in this misunderstood worship, his
presence is known and experienced.

He is here as he promised, in our midst. He lives not only
here but out in the world. He belongs to the future and calls
us into it in hope. He frees us from death and the drag of
the past. He goes before us into the world and calls us to
follow. Often, like the women at the tomb, we come prepared to stay with death. Sometimes we refuse his call to
follow and flee in fear. And sometimes we are perplexed
and afraid.

We are human, and the Easter Gospel narrative is written
for us. My friends, he is not in the tomb. He lives. He is not
constrained by the past. He goes before us into the future.
Do not sit around. Go! Do not be silent. Go and tell. He lives,
and so do you. Thanks be to God!

EASTER II 1985

Luke 24:36-49

For two weeks now we have been singing Easter hymns that
make declarations like "Jesus Christ is risen *today*!" and "He
is risen, he is risen. Tell it out with joyful voice!" These
hymns proclaim that something is happening today, right
now. We don't sing "Jesus Christ rose 1,955 years ago today," but "Christ is risen *today*." This is the happy morning;
this is the day of resurrection.

The hymn writers apparently thought the day of the
resurrection was right now. Strange thought number one.

In this service of the Lord's Supper, or Mass, or Holy

Communion, or Eucharist—whatever you wish to call it—
we assert that somehow and some way Jesus Christ is not
only risen but with us, right here and right now. We proclaim that, as he promised, where two or three are gathered
together in his name, he is in our midst. Orthodox Christians (Greek, Russian, and others) have a clear way of putting it. In their liturgy they say to one another, "Christ is in
our midst," with the reply, "He is and always will be."
Strange thought number two.

Easter, the day of resurrection, is today, right now. Christ
is in our midst. Two strange thoughts. Christians would
appear to be people who believe two unbelievable thoughts
before lunch.

A moment ago we heard read from this pulpit a strange
and unbelievable story, an Easter story told by Luke, which
may help us understand the two strange and unbelievable
thoughts I have just shared with you.

Listen to Luke's story of that first Easter. The eleven
disciples are gathered together with a few other followers of
the crucified Jesus. Without warning, Jesus himself is suddenly standing in the midst of them. The scene becomes
one of bewilderment and confusion. Luke says the disciples
are startled and terrified. They think they see a spirit. They
are troubled, questioning in their hearts. Perhaps they see
in the hands and feet of the person in their midst the marks
of the cross. Yet, says Luke, they disbelieve, but joyfully.
Literally, Luke says of this odd scene, "And while they still
disbelieved for joy, and wondered. . . ." They are troubled,
frightened, and joyfully disbelieving.

For troubled and perplexed Christians in 1985 who are
trying to make sense out of the Easter proclamation, does
Luke's strange story help or add to the confusion? I believe
it helps. Let me explain.

Luke says Jesus was in the midst of his disciples, yet they
did not recognize him. They supposed they saw a spirit. He
offered to show them his wounded hands and feet. They
were frightened and disbelieving, yet marveling and joyful.

This was no scientific demonstration. Their belief was not compelled; their senses were not overwhelmed by proof incontestable. No, his presence in their midst was ambiguous; it was an enigma, a mystery. They could disbelieve and be joyful at the same time. They could be simultaneously frightened and reassured by his presence.

For me this story is a great relief, a source of great comfort. He is risen today, and he is here in our midst—no less ambiguously and no less mysteriously than in that Easter gathering that Luke depicts. He leaves room for disbelief and space for pondering. How much more exciting and inviting is this marvelous mystery than some sterile proposition called "belief in the resurrection." His Easter presence with us is marveled at before it is reasoned about.

Perhaps the Easter presence is too good to be true, too marvelous for words, too startling for belief, too joyful for sobriety. I hope it is all this for you. It was for Luke. Luke invites us to perceive it fully. He says, "See it; open your eyes to behold and see."

Open your eyes, but open your minds as well. The Present Lord says, "These are my words which I spoke to you . . . that everything written about me in the law of Moses and the prophets and the psalms must be fulfilled. Then he opened their minds to understand the scriptures. . . ." The Scriptures that we read, old and new, are about him. The Scriptures that we preach concern him. When their meaning is opened to us, when they are understood, he is present, and our hearts burn within us. He both fulfills and interprets Scripture. He is present in the Word read and preached. Luke invites us to open our minds and hear the words of Jesus.

The Easter presence is seeing and hearing, eyes and minds opened. But it is much, much more. It is going and doing. According to Luke, we are called by the Lord Jesus to be "witnesses of these things," not just to see and hear but to do. We are to be witnesses to what we have seen and heard, and the Greek word for "witness" is literally "martyr." We are to be "martyrs"—active, energetic, risk-taking, perhaps even suffering witnesses to what we have beheld, to what our minds have grasped.

Luke's Easter story continues: "Repentance and forgiveness of sins should be preached in his name to all nations. . . ." Our witness involves telling the story of the Easter presence to all nations, literally all "ethnics," all groups, all races, all peoples. It involves not only telling the story but acting on it by preaching repentance and forgiveness in his name, by calling others to repentance for their participation in an unjust world.

If his Easter presence has caused us to turn away from injustice and toward the path of justice ("turning away" being the true meaning of "repentance"), then we are to help others to turn away and turn around also. This necessitates proclaiming his forgiveness as well. As we have been forgiven, we who are witnesses to the Easter presence are agents of his forgiveness in the world.

We see and hear, repent and are forgiven. We go and tell, calling others to repent, forgiving others in his name. He is present in our midst, in our telling and in our forgiving.

We are witnesses to his presence, startled by him, disbelieving for joy and full of wonder. Yet we witness, not out of arrogant, superior certainty, but with marveling disbelief. We behold his presence, and we hear something else—his promise: "Behold, I send the promise of my Father upon you . . . (you will be) clothed with power from on high."

The Easter presence is fulfilled by an Easter promise. He is risen today! He is in our midst. He fills us with his power. He promises to remain with us. His presence and his promise are too good to be true. The cry "He is in our midst; he is and will be" is too marvelous for belief. It causes both joy and disbelief. Yet it is as he promised, and his promise can be trusted. That is a matter of experience, joyful and frightening experience, experience of his awesome presence and power.

Saint Luke's saying that we will "be clothed with power,"

the power of his presence, reminds me of the way we talk when we say, "He put on a Marine uniform and had a new sense of pride in himself. He was filled with the spirit of the corps," or "He put on the uniform of a champion and played like a champion." To trust in his promise is to be clothed with the power of forgiveness and the humility of repentance. To trust in his promise is to know that he won't abandon us despite our bewilderment and disbelief.

He is risen! He is here! Open your eyes to see his presence. Open your minds to understand his word. He is in our midst! "O Lord of all, with us abide in this our joyful Eastertide." He promises to clothe us with his power. Turn around and accept his forgiveness. He is present; go and witness to others by your word and by your forgiveness. "He is risen, he is risen. Tell it out with joyful voice!"

THE SUNDAY AFTER ASCENSION 1985

One of the most troublesome phrases in the creed for me is "he ascended into heaven." Does it trouble you? It conjures up in my mind bad church art: Jesus in white, standing on a cloud and waving to his disciples who are standing on a mountaintop—or, worse still, a stained-glass window showing a cloud with two feet sticking out of the bottom. This is the Sunday after Ascension Day, and here we are hearing about the ascension. What are we to make out of it? Can we make any sense at all of a purported event in which our Lord was bodily carried from sight up and away from earth and apparently into outer space?

We have just heard Saint Luke's two narratives of the departure of Jesus, one from Bethany (found at the very end of Luke's Gospel) and one from the Mount of Olives (found in the first chapter of the Book of Acts). Let us look at them.

In both stories Jesus departs from his disciples, and in some textual versions the departure is described in similar language: he is taken or carried up into heaven. He departs; he is lifted up; he is taken from them. The point—if we can get away from the spatial metaphor, and I believe we should—is that by God's action, Jesus of the earthly ministry, Jesus of the agonizing death on the cross, is no longer to be present in a form that can be perceived by the senses.

However the glorified Lord of the Easter appearance is to be conceived, the appearances come to an end. According to Luke, there came a time—he says after forty days—when the special appearances of the Risen Lord came to a close. One era came to a close, and another came into being. That which we call the ascension is the dividing line between the era of Jesus on earth and the era of the Holy Spirit in the church. It was necessary, the Gospel writers tell us, that the earthly ministry of Jesus come to a close in order that his Spirit could be present to humankind everywhere. The narratives of the departure at Bethany and at the Mount of Olives point forward to his presence among us, to the presence of his Spirit with us; they do not look back. That is their point. Let us look at them more closely.

In Luke's story in Acts the disciples are left gaping into the sky. Two men in white address them: "Men of Galilee, why do you stand looking into heaven?" This reminds me of another scene in Luke. The women come to the tomb looking for the dead body of Jesus, and again two men in white ask a question: "Why do you seek the living among the dead?" Jesus our Lord, Jesus who taught and healed and was crucified and died for us, is not to be found in the graveyard among the dead. He lives.

Jesus is not to be found in the sky, seated on a cloud or dwelling on an asteroid. He is with us. Don't search among the dusty relics of the past nor among the constellations of the heavens. He is not down there (in the grave) or back there (in the past) or up there (in space). He is with us and among us, not among the dead but the living. Don't stand looking skyward. He is not coming on Halley's Comet. He is alive, here and now in our midst.

Our collect for this Sunday includes this prayer: "Mercifully give us faith to perceive that, according to his promise, he abides with his church on earth even to the end of the ages." That is our prayer and our claim and our hope.

"Why do you seek the living among the dead? Why do you stand looking into heaven?" It is the curse of much contemporary religion that it looks for Jesus primarily in the past. The Bible becomes the locus of Jesus. We read Scripture to find Jesus in its pages alone rather than to point to his presence in our midst. Nazareth, not Washington, becomes the place to meet him. We are right to seek Jesus in the pages of Scripture, but we shouldn't stop there. The ascension proclaims that he is a here-and-now Christ, in our world and in this place, in the midst of the faithful and with the person in need who accepts a glass of water given in the name of the Lord.

Much contemporary religion looks for Jesus primarily in the sky. It is heaven-oriented. For some sky-watching Christians, this world is evil and beyond transformation. Life is to be lived with eyes and hands upraised. This world is to be avoided as much as possible. Christians are right to avoid the corruption of this world but wrong to deny the possibility of its transformation. At least we should give it a try.

For others with their eyes fixed on heaven, this world has little to do with the world above or the world to come. The two worlds are distinct and separate; neither penetrates the other. The church is a bit of heaven, a place to which to retreat, but it has no transforming responsibility toward this world. Church and politics don't mix. The workplace and the church are isolated from one another, each with its own set of rules.

These sky-watching Christians find it easy to accept a dog-eat-dog economic environment while living in a warm, loving, but separate church environment. I find little to agree with here. "Men of Galilee, why do you stand looking into heaven?" Look instead into your unemployed brother's eye. See the malnourished child. Look toward the least of these his brethren.

This brings me to the promise—the second element in

Luke's stories of the departure of the Lord from his disciples. To them and to us he says, "Behold, I send the promise
of my Father upon you. . . . You shall receive power when
the Holy Spirit has come upon you." His promise, the Father's promise, is that we will be empowered by the Holy
Spirit, "clothed with power from on high."

We know from reading the Acts of the Apostles that the
disciples looked back to earth, that they left that mountaintop and plunged into the cities, where they taught and
healed and proclaimed the good news by word and deed.
They were so filled with power that skeptics said they were
drunk. They stood up to angry crowds, irate religious leaders, and cynical magistrates. Simple, uneducated men and
women were filled with the power to speak to multitudes,
and men who had fled the cross had the courage to die for
their faith. They were clothed with power. They heard and
accepted the promise and shared it with others.

As the departing Christ promised the disciples spiritual
power, he commissioned them: "You shall be my witnesses
(literally 'martyrs') in Jerusalem and in all Judea and Sa-
maria and to the end of the earth." The empowerment was
not only for personal growth, though that is important. It
was not only to build up the church, though that is necessary. The departing Christ filled them with power so that
others might know of the Christ and might have life in his
name. They and we are empowered so that the world may
believe in Jesus whom we call Lord and enjoy the abundant
life that he gives.

The promise is fulfilled as we come down from the
mountaintop into Jerusalem, into the city where a world in
need is to be found. If we stand frozen on Mount Olivet,
eyes glued to the clouds, we will miss our brothers and
sisters in need, and we will never really be clothed with the
power of the spirit. Christians may need to retreat from the
world; we all can use a mountaintop experience from time
to time. But we can't stay there. The power of that experience soon dissipates if we do not turn again to the world for
which he died.

I have just returned from Pittsburgh. It is a city of contrasts. A new city center gleams at the convergence of the three rivers; nearby are miles of idle, rusting steel plants. Downtown Pittsburgh is a hive of activity and renewal. But only a few miles away the Monongahela Valley has many thousands idle, vast numbers losing their homes, and increasing rates of suicide, divorce, and alcoholism.

Many Christians in Pittsburgh (and elsewhere, for that matter) proclaim a Christianity that has nothing to say to the thousands of unemployed except "Bear your suffering in silence. Technology has passed you by." This brand of religion does not urge the converted to transform a society that plunges hardworking men and women into idleness and despair. It preaches only a mountaintop religion, eyes fixed on the heavens, feet planted firmly inside the church. It has little to proclaim to either management or labor in the present crisis.

But there is another Christianity in Pittsburgh as well. It has left Olivet for Jerusalem. It has joined the dispossessed amid the rusting factory hulks. It is Catholic as well as Protestant. It is evangelical and sacramental. It has followed Christ into the world. It seeks him among the living and the dying, but in the present, not the past. It seeks to promote dialogue between management and labor, and it dares to presume to criticize the closing of industry and the impoverishment of thousands.

It seeks to transform, not to condemn, to transform systems and structures as well as individuals. It deserves the name evangelical. Its successes are modest, but the laity and clergy involved in the several Monongahela Valley ministries are trying to follow Christ into the world. They do not seek him among the dead or in the clouds but in the world. Your experience and my experience may not be the same as that of Christians in Pittsburgh, but the calling is the same for Christians everywhere: to follow Christ into his world, in the spirit of his ascension.

We are gathered here this morning to proclaim his ascension, to celebrate the truth of his presence among us and to return to the world in his name, empowered by his Spirit. We are here with his promise ringing in our ears. We are here praying, "Mercifully give us faith to perceive that, according to his promise, he abides with his church to the end of the ages." And perceiving his presence among us and accepting his promise, we are called to transform the world, looking not back to the tomb or up into the sky but into the eyes of our brothers and sisters for whom he died.

Works Consulted

Betz, Hans Dieter. "The Origin and Nature of Christian Faith According to the Emmaus Legend (Luke 24:13-32)." *Interpretation* 23 (1969): 32-46.

Bode, Edward L. *The First Easter Morning: The Gospel Accounts of the Women's Visit to the Tomb of Jesus*. Rome: Biblical Institute Press, 1970.

Bornkamm, Gunther. *Jesus of Nazareth*. Trans. Irene and Fraser McCluskey. New York: Harper & Brothers, 1960.

———. "The Risen Lord and the Earthly Jesus—Mt. 28:16-20," in *The Future of Our Religious Past: Essays in Honor of Rudolf Bultmann*. Trans. Charles E. Carlston. Ed. James M. Robinson. New York: Harper & Row, 1970.

Brown, Raymond E. *The Gospel According to John XIII-XXI*. Anchor Bible, vol. 29A. Garden City, N.Y.: Doubleday, 1970.

Buber, Martin. *Moses*. Oxford: East & West Library, 1946.

Carlston, Charles E. "Transfiguration and Resurrection." *Journal of Biblical Literature* 80 (1961): 233-40.

Conzelmann, Hans. *First Corinthians: A Critical and Historical Commentary on the Bible*. Trans. James W. Leitch. Ed. George W. MacRae. Philadelphia: Fortress Press, 1975.

Countryman, L. William. "Tertullian and the Regula Fidei." *Second Century* 2 (1982): 208-27.

Craig, William Lane. "The Guard at the Tomb." *New Testament Studies* 30 (1984): 273-81.

Cullmann, Oscar. *Early Christian Worship*. London: SCM Press, 1953.

———. *Immortality of the Soul or Resurrection of the Dead?* New York: Macmillan, 1965.

Dahl, M. E. *The Resurrection of the Body: A Study of I Corinthians 15*. Studies in Biblical Theology, no. 36. London: SCM Press, 1962.

Delorme, Jean. "The Resurrection and Jesus' Tomb: Mark 16, 1-8 in the Gospel Tradition," in *The Resurrection and Modern Biblical Thought*. Ed. P. DeSurgy. New York: Corpus Books, 1970.

Dillon, Richard J. *From Eye-Witnesses to Ministers of the Word: Tradi-*

tion and Composition in Luke 24. Rome: Biblical Institute Press, 1978.

Dodd, C. H. "The Appearances of the Risen Christ: An Essay in Form-Criticism of the Gospels," in *More New Testament Studies.* Grand Rapids: Eerdmans, 1968.

Dunn, James D. G. *Jesus and the Spirit: A Study of the Religious and Charismatic Experience of Jesus and the First Christians as Reflected in the New Testament.* Philadelphia: Westminster Press, 1975.

DuPont, Jacques. "The Meal at Emmaus," in *The Eucharist in the New Testament.* London: Geoffrey Chapman, 1965.

Ehrhardt, Arnold. "The Disciples of Emmaus." *New Testament Studies* 10 (1963-64): 182-201.

Ellis, I. P. "But Some Doubted." *New Testament Studies* 14 (1967-68): 574-80.

Evans, C. F. *Resurrection and the New Testament.* Studies in Biblical Theology, n.s., no. 12. London: SCM Press, 1970.

Fiorenza, Elisabeth Schüssler. *In Memory of Her: A Feminist Theological Reconstruction of Christian Origins.* New York: Crossroad, 1983.

Fitzmyer, Joseph. *The Gospel According to Luke I-IX.* Anchor Bible, vol. 28. Garden City, N.Y.: Doubleday, 1981.

_____. "To Know Him and to Know the Power of His Resurrection," in *To Advance the Gospel: New Testament Essays.* New York: Crossroad, 1981.

_____. "Two Views of New Testament Interpretation." *Interpretation* 32 (1978): 309-13.

Frei, Hans W. *The Identity of Jesus Christ: The Hermeneutical Bases of Dogmatic Theology.* Philadelphia: Fortress Press, 1975.

Fuller, Daniel P. *Easter Faith and History.* Grand Rapids: Eerdmans, 1965.

Fuller, Reginald H. *The Formation of the Resurrection Narratives.* New York: Macmillan, 1971.

Gadamer, Hans-Georg. *Truth and Method.* New York: Seabury Press, 1975.

Galloway, Allan D. *Wolfhart Pannenberg.* Ed. H. D. Lewis. London: George Allen & Unwin, 1973.

George, A. "The Accounts of the Appearances to the Eleven from Luke 24,36-53," in *The Resurrection and Modern Biblical Thought.* Ed. P. DeSurgy. New York: Corpus Books, 1970.

Hick, John. *Death and Eternal Life.* New York: Harper & Row, 1976.

Hooke, S. H. *The Resurrection of Christ as History and Experience.* London: Darton, Longman & Todd, 1967.

Hoskyns, Edwyn Clement. *Crucifixion—Resurrection: The Pattern of the Theology and Ethics of the New Testament.* London: SPCK, 1981.

Hubbard, Benjamin J. *The Matthean Redaction of a Primitive Apostolic Commissioning: An Exegesis of Matthew 28:16-20.* Missoula, Mont.: Scholars Press, 1974.

Jeremias, Joachim. *The Eucharistic Words of Jesus.* New York: Macmillan, 1955.

———. *New Testament Theology.* Vol. 1: *The Proclamation of Jesus.* New York: Scribner's, 1971.

Kasper, Walter. *Jesus the Christ.* New York: Paulist Press, 1976.

Kingsbury, J. D. "The Composition and Christology of Matt. 28:16-20." *Journal of Biblical Literature* 93 (1974): 573-84.

Kunneth, Walter. *The Theology of the Resurrection.* London: SCM Press, 1965.

Lampe, G. W. H., and D. M. MacKinnon. *The Resurrection: A Dialog.* Philadelphia: Westminster Press, 1967.

Leaney, A. R. C. "The Resurrection Narratives in Luke 24:12-53." *New Testament Studies* 2 (1955-56): 110-14.

Leon-Dufour, X. "The Appearances of the Risen Lord and Hermeneutics," in *The Resurrection and Modern Biblical Thought.* Ed. P. DeSurgy. New York: Corpus Books, 1970.

Longstaff, T. R. W. "The Women at the Tomb: Matthew 28:1 Re-examined." *New Testament Studies* 27 (1980-81): 277-82.

McKenzie, David. *Wolfhart Pannenberg and Religious Philosophy.* Washington: University Press of America, 1980.

Malina, Bruce J. "The Literary Structure and Form of Matt. 28:16-20." *New Testament Studies* 17 (1970-71): 87-103.

Manek, Jindrich. "The Apostle Paul and the Empty Tomb." *Novum Testamentum* 2 (1956-57): 276-80.

Marshall, Alfred. *The RSV Interlinear Greek-English New Testament: The Nestle Greek Text with a Literal English Translation.* Grand Rapids: Zondervan, 1958.

Marxsen, Willi. *The Resurrection of Jesus of Nazareth.* Trans. Margaret Kohl. Philadelphia: Fortress Press, 1970.

Meier, John P. "Two Disputed Questions in Matthew 28:16-20." *Journal of Biblical Literature* 96 (1977): 407-24.

Michaelis, W. "horáō C2," in *TDNT.* Ed. Gerhard Kittel and Gerhard Friedrich. Trans. Geoffrey W. Bromiley. 9 vols. Grand Rapids: Eerdmans, 1967, 5: 358-59.

Moule, C. F. D. *The Birth of the New Testament*. Rev. ed. San Francisco: Harper & Row, 1982.

————. *The Origins of Christology*. Cambridge: Cambridge University Press, 1977.

————. "The Post-Resurrection Appearances in the Light of Festival Pilgrimages." *New Testament Studies* 4 (1957-58): 58-61.

Neirynck, Frans. "John and the Synoptics—The Empty Tomb Stories." *New Testament Studies* 30 (1983-84): 161-87.

Niebuhr, Richard R. *Resurrection and Historical Reason: A Study of Theological Method*. New York: Scribner's, 1957.

Pannenberg, Wolfhart. *Jesus—God and Man*. Philadelphia: Westminster Press, 1968.

Perkins, Pheme. *Resurrection: New Testament Witness and Contemporary Reflection*. Garden City, N.Y.: Doubleday, 1984.

Perrin, Norman. *The Resurrection According to Matthew, Mark and Luke*. Philadelphia: Fortress Press, 1977.

Ramsey, A. Michael. *The Resurrection of Christ*. Philadelphia: Westminster Press, 1946.

Ricoeur, Paul. *Hermeneutics and the Human Sciences*. Ed. John Thompson. Cambridge: Cambridge University Press, 1981.

Robinson, J. A. T. *The Body: A Study in Pauline Theology*. Studies in Biblical Theology, no. 5. London: SCM Press, 1952.

————. *Can We Trust the New Testament?* Grand Rapids: Eerdmans, 1977.

Robinson, James M. "Jesus: From Easter to Valentinus (or to the Apostles' Creed)." *Journal of Biblical Literature* 101 (1982): 5-37.

————, and John B. Cobb, eds. *Theology as History*. Vol. 3 of New Frontiers in Theology. New York: Harper & Row, 1967.

Shepherd, Massie H., Jr. *The Oxford American Prayer Book Commentary*. New York: Oxford University Press, 1950.

Sider, Ronald J. "The Pauline Conception of the Resurrection Body in I Cor. 15:35-54." *New Testament Studies* 21 (1974-75): 428-39.

Smith, Robert H. *The Easter Gospels: The Resurrection of Jesus According to the Four Evangelists*. Minneapolis: Augsburg, 1983.

Stendahl, Krister, ed. *Immortality and Resurrection: Ingersoll Lectures*. New York: Macmillan, 1971.

Torrance, Thomas F. *Space, Time and Resurrection*. Grand Rapids: Eerdmans, 1976.

Waetjen, Herman J. *The Origin and Destiny of Humanness.* San Rafael, Cal.: Omega Books, 1976.

Wilckens, Ulrich. *Resurrection: Biblical Testimony to the Resurrection—An Historical Examination and Explication.* Trans. A. M. Stewart. Atlanta: John Knox Press, 1978.

Wolff, Hans W. *Anthropology of the Old Testament.* Trans. Margaret Kohl. Philadelphia: Fortress Press, 1974.